OVERCOME

AI

*How to Build a Secure Financial
Future in the Age of Artificial
Intelligence*

SCOTT GAMM

n*b

NICHOLAS BREALEY
PUBLISHING

BOSTON · LONDON

First published in the United States of America in 2020
by Nicholas Brealey Publishing

An Hachette company

24 23 22 21 20 1 2 3 4 5 6 7 8

Library of Congress Control Number: 2020903661

ISBN 978-1-5293-6101-8
U.S. eBook ISBN 978-1-5293-3930-7
U.K. eBook ISBN 978-1-5293-6103-2

Printed in the United States of America

Nicholas Brealey Publishing policy is to use papers that are natural, renewable
and recyclable products and made from wood grown in sustainable forests. The
logging and manufacturing processes are expected to conform to the environmental
regulations of the country of origin.

Nicholas Brealey Publishing
Carmelite House
50 Victoria Embankment
London EC4Y 0DZ
Tel: 020 7122 6000

Nicholas Brealey Publishing
Hachette Book Group
53 State Street
Boston, MA 02109, USA
Tel: (617) 523 3801

www.nbuspublishing.com

About the Author

Scott Gamm is a Wall Street expert and founder of Strategy Voice Associates, LLC, a public relations and content strategy firm. He previously spent years as a financial journalist. At Yahoo Finance, he reported on the stock market and the economy. At TheStreet, he hosted a daily live stock market show with TheStreet's founder and CNBC host Jim Cramer.

As a journalist, Gamm has interviewed top CEOs and politicians such as Bridgewater Associates founder Ray Dalio, The Carlyle Group co-founder David Rubenstein, Carly Fiorina, Charles Schwab founder Charles Schwab, and former Ohio Governor John Kasich.

He has appeared as a commentator on NBC's *Today*, CNBC, MSNBC, Fox News, Fox Business Network, CBS News, ABC News, and C-SPAN, among other outlets.

Gamm is the author of *More Money, Please: The Financial Secrets You Never Learned in School* (Plume/Penguin Random House, 2013).

Gamm is a graduate of New York University's Stern School of Business.

Contents

1 Financial Independence and Artificial Intelligence   1

2 What Does Artificial Intelligence Mean for
the Gig Economy?   11

3 The Robots Determine How Much Money You
Need to Retire   23

4 How to Prepare for the "Artificial Intelligence Tax"   55

5 Debt and Robots Don't Mix   77

6 Understanding the Stock Market   95

7 What Artificial Intelligence May Mean
for 401(k)s   125

8 Real Estate and Financial Independence   133

9 Billionaires and Financial Independence   177

10 Conclusion   181

Endnotes   183

Index   193

Financial Independence and Artificial Intelligence

There are two important trends going on right now in society: financial independence and artificial intelligence. Chances are you have heard of both, but you probably haven't seen the two trends linked and analyzed so closely together. Understanding these two trends and how they are related can make or break your financial future, so you've picked up the right book.

But first, a question: Do you ever wake up in the morning wishing you didn't have to go to work? Even if you like your job—which most people don't—there are still days when all you want to do is lie in bed. You're not alone. Financial responsibilities, however, keep you clinging to your job. Without that paycheck, the rent won't be paid, your student loans will not be paid, and you won't be able to take that trip to Europe. But what if you had enough money to pay your monthly expenses without a traditional 9-to-5 job? What if you were financially independent? If this sounds appealing, read on. Before you get too excited, a few things:

1. I am by no means an advocate of you quitting your job so you can hang out on the beach all day. Sorry!
2. This book does not detail a get-rich-quick scheme. I have no secret formula for becoming an overnight millionaire. Read that sentence again.

What I do have is information that can change how you think about your finances. Because a lot of the financial rules you have been taught may not serve you so well for the next few decades. (I'll explain why in a moment.) Or maybe you've never really thought about money. If that's you, keep reading, because you'll be consuming this information with little or no preconceived notions of how money works or how to maximize your financial future. Also, don't think of this book as a financial advice book. No one wants to be lectured and, believe me, while I've studied these topics for years and years, I'm in no position to tell you what to do with your money. You don't have to implement any of the information in this book. It's just information, and you will decide what to do with it.

First, let's address two important terms that are at the center of this book: financial independence and artificial intelligence. A thorough understanding of these terms should change the way you think about money for good. Allow me to explain: The financial independence movement is gaining attention, especially among young people in their twenties and thirties—the Millennials. Here's how it works: cut expenses, save nearly all of your income, and invest wisely. Within a certain number of years, you'll have enough money to quit your soul-sucking 9-to-5 job and retire—or at least pursue a passion, even if it doesn't pay much. When I say "enough money," that is a subjective term. It depends on your lifestyle, how much money you need to live, and, perhaps more important, where you plan to live for the foreseeable future, because the cost of living varies widely, not just within the United States but also around the world. A key component of the "enough money" concept is having a mountain of assets (this could be cash, stocks, or real estate rental properties) that produces enough income to cover your monthly expenses. Some call this *passive income*—or income that you don't have to do much work to receive. It is income that you receive without having to show up to a 9-to-5 job. Granted, it can take years and even decades to build up this mountain of assets, but in a nutshell that's what financial independence is: you're not dependent on a job, a career, a company, a paycheck, or a boss. That doesn't mean you stop working when you achieve financial independence. But it does mean that if you get fired from the job, you won't face financial ruin or a pressing need to find a job the next day to keep paying your bills. We'll be delving into the different types of financial independence later on in this book. But, generally speaking, having enough money to pay for your life without receiving a regular salary is what I'm talking about when I say financial independence.

As such, many young people are ditching the "retire at age 65" path that their parents and grandparents followed. They're tired of being chained to a desk all day in an over-air-conditioned office building located in a soulless office park facing a highway. They want freedom *now*. And money provides freedom. It sounds like a pipe dream, right? If you're saddled with student loan and credit card debt and can barely afford to pay rent, how can you possibly think of retiring at age 30, let alone 65? Whether it's at age 28 or 38, the notion of retiring super early (i.e., decades before age 65, the typical retirement age) is not a fantasy. While it doesn't happen overnight, you don't have to win the lottery and you don't have to start the next trillion-dollar tech company (although either would help!). You just have to make sacrifices and establish a smart investing strategy, which we'll talk about later.

What Is Artificial Intelligence?

An important concept that makes achieving financial independence even more urgent is artificial intelligence. The keyword here is *urgent*. So many people want to have a lot of money in the bank. But many times we procrastinate the notion of saving money because we think we have many years to build up our mountain of assets—why start scrimping now? Why maximize our 401(k) contribution when we can instead use that money for a cruise to the Caribbean? You see, I'm interpreting the financial independence movement in a different way than you may understand it. I realize that many young people may dislike their jobs and dread the Monday morning alarm clock. I know that having a few million dollars in the bank (or even $1 million!) would allow many people to quit their 9-to-5 job and pursue a lower-paying passion. But that job you hate may not even be around in 5 years, 10 years, or 15 years, thanks to robots that can do your job better than you can. A fancy term for robots is artificial intelligence. Herein lies the linkage between financial independence and artificial intelligence that I mentioned earlier. Here are some ways robots can be more appealing than human workers:

- They can be cheaper
- They can work faster
- They don't get sick
- They don't ask for vacation or time off
- They don't complain
- They don't browse social media or dating apps while at work

What employer wouldn't want to replace human workers with robots? Don't just take my word for it. The smartest minds in business are already talking about technology's effects on the job market. In a December 2018 blog post, businessman Richard Branson wrote[1] the following:

New innovations will drive industries forward, but they will also reduce our reliance on people power. Ideas such as driverless cars and more advanced drones are becoming a reality, and machines will be used for more and more jobs in the future.

It's extremely hard to tell how artificial intelligence or broader technological advancement will affect the future of work. Do a quick internet search on this topic and you will find a cacophony of different viewpoints. Some say artificial intelligence will kill jobs. Others say it will create new ones. Take "The Future of Jobs Report 2018" from the World Economic Forum: the report concludes that by 2025 over half of tasks performed in the workplace will be completed by machines versus 29 percent currently.[2] It goes on to assert:

> Such a transformation will have a profound effect on the global labour force, however in terms of overall numbers of new jobs the outlook is positive, with 133 million new jobs expected to be created by 2022 compared to 75 million that will be displaced.[3]

From a global perspective, that's encouraging news: the World Economic Forum expects that machines will actually create jobs. But what does it mean for individuals? If you're one of the 75 million workers who will be displaced, will you be eligible for one of the 132 million jobs that will be created? The uncertainty is crippling. You can't plan your life based on a forecast, a report, or some expert's opinion. But let's rationally ponder the possible outcomes from the rise of artificial intelligence and technology: Could artificial intelligence eliminate jobs? Yes. Could artificial intelligence spark underemployment—where people end up working in a much lower-paying job that is not commensurate with their education level or experience? Yes. Could artificial intelligence force people to become reskilled and retrained in new technologies? Yes, says IBM. In a September 2019 press release discussing an IBM Institute for Business Value (IBV) study, the company said some 120 million people may need to learn new skills to keep up with artificial intelligence: "The study showed that new skills requirements are rapidly emerging, while other skills are becoming obsolete."[4]

How Big Companies Are Preparing for Artificial Intelligence and the Future of Work

If you're still not convinced on the changing nature of the workplace, consider this: well-known companies are investing big sums of money in retraining their workers. In July 2019, Amazon announced[5] plans to spend $700 million to retrain 100,000 US employees for jobs that are expected to increase in demand, such as machine learning, robotics, and cloud computing, among others. Global consulting and accounting firm PwC is spending $3 billion over several years on upskilling its employees.[6] Financial firm JPMorgan Chase in March 2019 revealed plans to spend $350 million on a five-year plan to "prepare for the future of work and meet the growing demand for skilled workers," the company said in a press release.[7] I could go on and on with examples of some of the most well-known companies like these announcing multimillion- and multibillion-dollar plans to retrain their workers. These examples illustrate that big companies recognize the changing workforce so much so that they're willing to invest big sums of money to prepare for the shift. This is great if you work for one of these companies. They're trying to help make the transition to a world driven by artificial intelligence and technology a little more palatable. But if you don't work at a company with the resources to help prepare you, it's time to take matters into your own hands. That's what this book is about. You may eventually decide to go back to school or spend money to invest in your own education to prepare yourself for the future of work. That education likely requires a hefty out-of-pocket expense. All the more reason to alter your financial plan now, while you have a job, to prepare for the investment you might make in yourself to learn new skills in 5 years, 10 years, or even 20 years.

The artificial intelligence revolution and the worry surrounding what it means for people's ability to stay employed even made its way into the 2020 presidential race in the United States. Believe me, this book is not about politics, but during the race several candidates, most notably entrepreneur Andrew Yang, made the changing nature of the workforce a key pillar of their political campaigns. On his website,[8] Yang outlined his proposal to create a new Department of Technology in the US government with a cabinet-level position of secretary of technology. Here's what the campaign said:[9]

> We need to have government hand-in-hand with technologists to make sure that we fully understand the impact of AI and other innovations before they're widely adopted in different settings.

Even US presidential candidates, Yang in particular, recognize the importance of artificial intelligence and its uncertain possible impact on society in the coming decades. The elevation of artificial intelligence to this presidential level of discourse is proof that leaders are starting to take technology's potential threat to jobs seriously. After all, it's the government that has the power to regulate and potentially slow the implementation and adoption of any job-killing technology.

How Artificial Intelligence May Affect Specific Industries

You might think your job is immune to artificial intelligence. After all, you may have spent hundreds of thousands of dollars on a fancy business degree.

Do you work in finance now? If so, you're probably making a nice salary. In 2017, Deutsche Bank CEO John Cryan told the *Financial Times* that a "big number" of his 97,000 employees would lose their jobs amid the rise of technology: "The truthful answer is we won't need as many people," he said.[10]

My point is, artificial intelligence may not just be a threat to cashiers making minimum wage. (Have you seen the self-checkout kiosks at a drugstore or in the supermarket?) People in highly paid industries—many of whom have fancy and expensive academic degrees—may also be at risk. Again, this isn't my opinion. I'm not the CEO of a major institution. I'm just reporting on what these CEOs and business leaders have said. They decide how many employees will work at their company. If they are sounding the alarm on artificial intelligence, we should at least be aware of this and, at best, consider taking action to prepare for this changing work dynamic. That's what this book aims to help you accomplish: an understanding of the trends that will inspire you to change your thinking *and* your finances. Ultimately, it's up to you to decide how seriously to take the artificial intelligence threat and whether or not to take action to bolster your finances to prepare for it.

Quick Review

Here are a few key items to remember from chapter 1:

1. Financial independence means having a mountain of assets that will produce enough income to cover your monthly expenses. This is a core concept of this book and will be covered extensively in almost every chapter.
2. Just because you have achieved financial independence, that doesn't necessarily mean you will stop working and retire. It means you will be less reliant on a "conventional" 9-to-5 job for survival.
3. The rise of artificial intelligence and its potential to kill jobs makes achieving financial independence all the more urgent.
4. If you think artificial intelligence's threat to jobs is overblown, that's fine. But look at what top business leaders, politicians, and companies are saying and doing about it. That is your clue.

What Does Artificial Intelligence Mean for the Gig Economy?

We are living in a new economy. You don't need to have a 9-to-5 job to make a decent living anymore. Thanks to technology and the internet, you can work when you want, for how long you want, and, in some cases, still be able to pay your bills.

This idea has been widely described as the "gig economy." This is where you take a job here and a job there and at the end of the month you may have earned money that is equivalent to what you would earn by sitting in an air conditioned office for a 40-hour workweek. The problem with this strategy is that there is uncertainty on the quantity and frequency of gigs. Some weeks you may have more gigs than you can handle, while other weeks may become a struggle. In the end, it may balance out, but a job in the gig economy doesn't come with that steady paycheck every week that a 9-to-5 job offers.

Now let's be clear: the only thing certain about a 9-to-5 job is the amount of your paycheck. Your salary remains the same, with the exception of occasional raises, bonuses, or commissions. But that base salary is a number you know. What isn't stable about the 9-to-5 job is that the employer can lay you off at any time. So at any moment, your "certain" paycheck could go away.

There is also a hybrid model: where you keep your 9-to-5 job for the stability but take on some side projects thanks to the gig economy. This can be a viable way to earn some extra money on the side to get to the 60 percent savings rate I keep talking about.

When you think of the gig economy, chances are, you think of Uber and Lyft. If you own a car, the idea is you can turn on the app and start making money by driving people around. You can treat it like a full-time job or just drive on the weekends. There is flexibility. There are many other types of gig economy companies and platforms outside of driving. There are platforms where you can take on various freelance work, including writing, copyediting, computer coding, graphic design—you name it!

The gig economy has become such a widespread phenomenon that even Wall Street has taken notice in a big way. In 2019, both Uber and Lyft went public, meaning shares of these two companies are now sold to the public.

The idea of a company going public is a major milestone in business. As of January 2020, the outstanding value of Uber's stock stood at $58 billion.[1] The outstanding value of Lyft's stock, also as of January 2020, was $14 billion.[2] That's roughly $70 billion in market capitalization assigned to just two companies that widely represent the gig economy. The entrance of Uber and Lyft into the capital markets space is a clear endorsement of the staying power that these kinds of companies may have—or at least the excitement around this industry among members of the investing community.

But could artificial intelligence disrupt the gig economy, which was built on technology? Uber and Lyft would not be possible without smartphones and the wide use of technology among consumers. Could *already* technologically advanced services be disrupted? And what does that mean for workers who rely on income from completing jobs from these services? Here, we're talking about the rise of self-driving or autonomous vehicles. In fact, Uber is taking steps to develop self-driving car technology and says this on its website: "We want to bring self-driving vehicles to the Uber network around the world."[3]

What will happen to the drivers who rely on the ride sharing apps for income? Will they be displaced? And for today's Millennials, is relying on income from the gig economy a sound strategy if the sector is ripe for disruption from artificial intelligence?

These questions are difficult to answer because the issues involve a high degree of speculation. For more information on this, I decided to turn to an expert on the gig economy: Arun Sundararajan, a professor at New York University's Stern School of Business and author of

The Sharing Economy: The End of Employment and the Rise of Crowd-Based Capitalism, which explores some of the themes of the gig economy.

Professor Sundararajan was kind enough to talk to me about how artificial intelligence may affect the gig economy. I think you'll be interested to hear his take on this and what he's advising students in his business school classes to do to prepare for all of this technological and societal change. Here below is an excerpt from my conversation with him:[4]

★ ★ ★

Scott Gamm: Is artificial intelligence going to be a problem for the gig economy and those workers?

Professor Sundararajan: Over a long enough period of time—over the next 10 to 20 years—there will be a substitution of Uber and Lyft drivers and of DoorDash, Postmates, and Grubhub delivery people. A lot of these services are going to rely more and more on robotic and artificial intelligence–driven capabilities rather than humans. Now, that comes with the following caveats: First off, the pace at which these platform services are growing may end up leading to more work through the platform rather than less, as artificial intelligence starts to kick in. For example, you are not going to have a robot that does everything from start to finish as far as the delivery of your food goes. The change is going to be incremental. There will be portions of the delivery that might be handled by a self-driving car or a sidewalk robot. That in turn is going to lower the costs of these services, and that cost decrease will increase the demand for the service among consumers. That will induce a demand for more and more of the humans involved in the process of carrying out these delivery services. Sometimes when the cost of something goes down and it's not completely substituted by the artificial intelligence or robotics technology, the demand for human labor can actually go up and not down because of the expansion of the market. The idea that in five years all of the Uber drivers are going to be unemployed because the cars are all going to be driving themselves is wishful thinking. We're looking at at least a decade, to me. If self-driving cars get to a technological capability in a few years that is satisfactory to the public in that they cause fewer car accidents, for example, there are a whole bunch of other forces that determine whether a technology that can do something ends up doing it. The idea that just because the technology can do something means it's going to start doing that immediately is flawed. There are political factors too. One self-driving car or truck that is driven into a building in an attack, for example, could set back the whole industry by 10 years independent of the capabilities of the technology. The specter of unemployed truck drivers could cause political resistance to allowing self-driving trucks unmanned on the road. Labor resistance can cause pushback. You have to think about all of these different factors together in trying to make an estimate for when the artificial intelligence will really start to substitute for the humans. It will be much faster in factories, where it's all about efficiency and there's not a lot of consumer acceptance. But in a consumer-facing setting, where societal acceptance is a big part of the equation, there's a pretty big gap between 'the technology can do this' and 'we're going to see a widespread adoption of the technology.'

In the very long run, yes, all driving will be fully autonomous, but that's at least a couple of decades away. For food delivery services, I think the change will be a little faster on the adoption of artificial intelligence, but it'll also be more incremental and so this could lead to an increase in demand for human labor in the short-term.

Scott Gamm: When we hear experts say artificial intelligence could hurt employment in some areas and create jobs in other areas, what is the end result for society? Won't there be winners and losers in this?

Professor Sundararajan: There are always winners and losers with technological progress. This is something that we've seen happen for centuries. Since the early mechanization of labor, there are certain types of work that gets displaced and become less valuable and society then collectively in some ways redeploys human labor to things the machines can't do well.

The short answer is yes, there will be winners and losers. I think the thing that makes people worried is that the advances in artificial intelligence are cognitive—about perception and cognition—which we always thought were the exclusive domain of humans beings. So there is this feeling that if computers can think for us, what is left for humans to do? But this is historically something that humans have always worried about. When the machines were deployed during the first industrial revolution, in the early nineteenth century and the late eighteenth century in England, the workers thought, *What is going to be left for humans to do?* Over time, work starts to get redefined.

I look at what I do for work: I educate people, I write, speak, I do research, I have conversations. Two hundred years ago, this would not have been considered work—it would be leisure. Work was something that you did physically. Our whole conception of what are productive activities that lead to someone being able to earn a living from it seems to have changed quite significantly over time as machines have started to do some of the things that humans used to do. I don't see any reason why this time is going to be substantially different.

Scott Gamm: What advice do you give to your students about how to prepare for all of this change?

Professor Sundararajan: I'm telling them to expect that they will have to change occupations at least once in their careers. It used to be, two generations ago, you imagined getting a job and never switching jobs. Now, switching jobs has become the norm. But switching occupations is still not common. I think for the next generation, switching occupations is likely to be common.

Whatever business or profession you are entering, build capabilities to be an entrepreneur. You may not start the next billion-dollar business, but you have to think like an entrepreneur; you have to build a network. You have to know how to be nimble, and you have to invest in design thinking. You have to be able to not just be good at something in a way that plugs into an organizational machine and climbs the corporate ladder, but you have to be able to shape your own reality and think more broadly about large, unstructured problems. The idea of joining Goldman Sachs as an investment banker or Procter & Gamble as an analyst, for example, and climbing the corporate ladder to president of the division or company—that's not going to be the traditional career trajectory [in 10 or 20 years]. A lot of people are going to have to take stock at some point and say,

"What's next?"—not just in terms of shifting jobs but in terms of reinventing themselves completely.

It's about being able to think broadly like that and in some ways reimagine what you could be. The best subjects and the best things that are taught in business schools today that prepare someone for this are classes about entrepreneurship. You don't learn this in a finance, marketing, or operations class, but you come close to learning this in an entrepreneurship class and so I nudge students in that direction.

Scott Gamm: With starting a business, it's not so cookie-cutter as it is in a corporate job, where you're sitting there waiting for the next promotion.

Professor Sundararajan: And, you have to go out and network—you have to be able to decide something, believe in it, go out and prove it.

★ ★ ★

I learned so much by speaking with Professor Sundararajan and I hope you did too. I was struck by his differentiation between the capabilities of a technology and its actual implementation: that just because a technology can do something, doesn't mean that something will be translated into reality. There is a gray area. Plus, the technology may have to be filtered through political and societal checkpoints before it is fully implemented. I think this is an important point and this angle should make us all feel a little bit better about technology's possible job displacement over the next few decades. That's not to say that we shouldn't watch the technological trends as it pertains to the future of work (you're clearly watching them, otherwise you wouldn't have picked up this book). But thinking about these political and societal checkpoints may help to lessen your anxiety about the future of work. I also think his point about the evolution of work is incredibly important. Professor Sundararajan is an accomplished professor and author and yet even he admits that the core pillars of his job would not be considered work a few centuries ago. What I took from that part of the interview was that there are jobs that could come about in 10 or 20 years that we may have never even heard of today. Think about that for a moment: there is a chance that the company or job you may have in 10 or 20 years hasn't even been created or invented yet.

And that is a great segue into my favorite part of my interview with Professor Sundararajan: his advice for business school students. I wanted to ask him about this because if you are a student or a young person, you are going to be at prime working age in 10, 20, or 30 years when this artificial intelligence technology is expected to become mainstream. The fact that Professor Sundararajan thinks the next generation will need to change occupations during their career is incredible. Climbing the corporate ladder may not be a feasible trajectory anymore.

This is quite a scary topic: that you might need to change occupations in twenty years. There are so many questions here such as:

- Will you be qualified for an occupational change?
- Will the pay be enough to support yourself?
- Will you need to invest in new training and learn new skills to prepare for an occupational shift?

Professor Sundararajan's analysis sums up how times are changing. You used to be able to stay at the same company for your entire career, but that's rare these days. Today, people are constantly changing jobs and entering new career fields. In the future, according to Professor Sundararajan, occupational change should become more common.

Occupational Change and Financial Independence

How does Professor Sundararajan's thesis about occupational change relate to financial independence? Let's say you do have to change occupations in the next few years or decades. Does the thought of this make your stomach churn? Even if occupational change becomes a "normal" phenomenon—it can still be a stressful process. What scares most people about occupational change is the uncertainty. What if the change doesn't happen immediately? What if that occupational change takes several years or results in a few years of a lower-paying job? What if the occupational change requires going back to school? That can be expensive.

Having a mountain of assets that is large enough to produce income that covers your monthly expenses helps ease the anxiety of any possible future occupational change.

Universal Basic Income

Speaking of how to grapple with costs associated with a change in your future occupation, universal basic income (UBI) comes to mind. This is essentially where the government would pay every citizen a fixed sum of money each month, say $1,000, just to cover basic monthly expenses.

I also asked Professor Sundararajan about UBI, and here is that part of my conversation with him.[5]

★ ★ ★

Scott Gamm: What do you think about universal basic income? It's often a topic that comes to mind when you think about artificial intelligence's possible displacement of jobs across the board.

Professor Sundararajan: I'm a very strong proponent of rebuilding and strengthening our social safety net. It's designed for a different economy—for a twentieth-century economy of full-time employment. We certainly need to make sure that there's a good safety net for people in the gig economy and freelancers, as well as provide more support for people who need to transition from one career to the next. However, I don't think universal basic income is the right solution. I often speak on panels at events on universal basic income and I'm usually the lone dissent on this—with other speakers talking about how wonderful it is. I chat with the audience after these events, and I find that most people who are excited by the idea of a universal basic income, if you drill down a little, are really excited about a stronger safety net. If we could harness the political capital to create a new social safety net program like a universal basic income (any decent universal basic income program in the United States is going to cost between $2 trillion and $3 trillion a year), we'd be creating a new public program that is of the scale of Social Security and Medicare. We spend $2 trillion a year on Social Security and Medicare put together. If we can actually create a universal basic income, that money would be much better spent on targeted programs, rather than on a universal basic income.

Quick Review

Discussing artificial intelligence tends to involve a bit of speculation, especially in terms of how the technology may or may not affect certain industries. But its potential affect on the gig economy is particularly interesting to me because the gig economy is such a new phenomenon. We typically hear about technology replacing old technologies, not new ones. Here are a few takeaways from the chapter:

1. Politicians have the power to slow the ripple effects of technology and its impact on jobs— even if the technological capability of a robot to replace a human worker exists.
2. Be prepared to change not just jobs in your career but occupations as well.

The Robots Determine How Much Money You Need to Retire

Have you noticed that a lot of game shows over the years have dazzled contestants with the idea of winning $1 million? There is something special about the number. It's got plenty of zeros: 1,000,000. And if you are making a five- or even low-six-figure salary, you don't need an advanced degree in economics to realize that it is going to take you years to save a million dollars. Yet lately, and maybe this is just me, I have noticed people scoff sometimes at the idea of a million dollars as not being a lot of money—that a million dollars doesn't go as far as it used to. And maybe that's true (you can barely even buy a one-bedroom apartment in New York City for $1 million), but, honestly, unless you have a million dollars already, you are in no position to scoff at the idea of saving a million dollars. I'm not saying that having a million dollars is enough to retire. It may not be. I'm just saying that a noble financial goal is to attain a mountain of assets worth $1 million. That doesn't mean you stop saving after achieving that goal, but getting to a million is a great foundation—a great first step. If you think that's way too ambitious of a goal to achieve, hopefully you'll have the information you need to view this goal in a more realistic light after reading this book. Because saving a million dollars (or more) is more attainable than you think.

The goal of this chapter is to educate you on how much money is needed to achieve financial independence. This is an incredibly difficult question because it involves so much conjecture. Even after reading this chapter, you may still have plenty of questions about how you will be able to achieve financial independence. Again, financial independence means having a mountain of assets that will produce enough income to cover your monthly expenses. The term "produces income" can mean a few things, such as:

- Your mountain of assets is in the form of stocks or stock funds that produce a certain amount of income each year in dividends. (I'll explain what dividends are later in the book.)
- Your mountain of assets is in the form of real estate rental investment properties that produce a certain profit each month that covers your personal monthly expenses.

Financial independence means you don't need to rely on a paycheck from your job to survive. A more comprehensive definition of financial independence is coming up in a moment, but keep this brief definition in mind for now. Anytime we talk about the future there is a high degree of speculation. We don't know what is going to happen tomorrow, in a month, in a year, or in a decade. This is especially true surrounding such a nuanced and complex topic like artificial intelligence and its impact on jobs. Maybe we are all worrying for nothing. I'll discuss later in the book what happens if artificial intelligence turns out to be a big nothing—if it's just all hype. But for now, I'm going to write through the lens of the worst-case scenario: that artificial intelligence is going to wipe away your job. With that, here are two of the most important questions to ask yourself:

1. When might I lose my job?
2. How much money do I need to have saved in order to cover my monthly expenses if/when I lose my job?

It is impossible for us to tell if or when your job will be taken from artificial intelligence or from some other reason (like a routine layoff). The reason artificial intelligence may be more of an issue than a routine layoff is because with artificial intelligence, we may be talking about a fundamental change in the nature of your job. You may not be able to find a new job so fast if robots completely replace your line of work and render your skills obsolete. Think about that for a second. What if no one wants or needs your skills anymore? Or maybe employers want your skills, but they can get away with paying you much less for those skills than, say, 10 or 20 years ago. And these are skills you probably spent decades honing. It's a scary prospect.

Currently, if you get laid off from your company, perhaps you could find a job at another employer within the same or a similar industry. But if your industry is relying more and more on robots to complete the tasks you once completed as an employee, how do you and your skills fit into the equation? That leaves you with a few bleak possibilities:

1. You are either out of luck (meaning you can't find the job you once had or something similar).
2. You have to learn new skills to put yourself in a position to be hired for the jobs that were not affected by artificial intelligence. Or this reskilling can allow you to potentially be hired for the new jobs that artificial intelligence might create. Remember the studies I mentioned in chapter 1 that talked about how artificial intelligence can create new types of jobs? It's certainly possible. But it's hard to tell what those jobs will be, what they would pay, and the level or duration of retraining efforts you would need to undergo to even be considered for those "new jobs." Retraining takes time and probably sizable sums of money.

Now let's be clear: retraining and reskilling are taking place right now at many big-name companies. What does that mean? Companies themselves see this shift as serious enough that they are willing to invest billions of dollars to prepare their existing workers. Or, in an even bleaker sense, artificial intelligence has yet to pose a major threat to jobs right now. The unemployment rate was only 3.5 percent, according to the Bureau of Labor Statistics[1] as of September 2019. While that's a very low unemployment rate by historical standards, unemployment increased significantly in 2020 amid the tragic COVID-19 outbreak. But that increase in unemployment was because of the economic shutdown stemming from the virus. The point is, the economy was strong before the virus and companies were still investing in reskilling, and they wouldn't be investing in it if they thought workers' skills were up to snuff. So if our skills aren't where they need to be now, before the artificial intelligence wave, what will our skill level be 5 or 10 years from now, when the artificial intelligence technology has had more time to develop and embeds itself into the economy? In other words, are the reskilling efforts moving fast enough? Faster than the pace of artificial intelligence development? It's a hard question to answer. I realize a lot of this is speculation, but these are important questions when we talk about reskilling.

Bottom line: reskilling can be a broader solution to the job threat artificial intelligence may pose. It's a nice soundbite; it's a nice talking point for politicians and CEOs to say on television. But it may not be a solution for you. Reskilling is risky. What if you don't take well to the new skills? What are you going to fall back on? What if you can't afford the costs associated with reskilling? A mountain of income-producing assets would help, right?

As mentioned in chapter 1, the next decade will be important for building the mountain of assets needed to become financially independent. Ten years is a reasonable period to start achieving this goal. Plus, it may be as many as 10 years before artificial intelligence becomes a meaningful threat to jobs. The impact could happen sooner than that or later, but let us approach this with a 10-year mindset. I titled this chapter "The Robots Determine How Much Money You Need to Retire" because it really depends on when (or if) the artificial intelligence threat hits your specific job. The longer it takes, the more time you would theoretically remain in your job and the more time you'll have to build up your mountain of assets.

The Ultimate Financial Equation

I want to delve deeper into the second question that was raised a few pages ago:

How much money do you need to have saved in order to cover your monthly expenses?

I'll say it again: the goal is to have a mountain of assets that produces enough income to cover your monthly expenses. The bigger the mountain, the more income that mountain can produce. But first, let's get granular!

At the center of personal finance is one key equation. I promise it's simple arithmetic. No need to dust off your old calculus textbooks.

Here it is:

Income − Expenses = Your Money

The result of this equation is personal profit. In fact, one of the basic tenets of finance is understanding the definition of *profit* (the money left over *after* expenses are paid).

Profit is *very* different from revenue. Revenue is the money a business makes *before* paying all of its expenses (expenses can include employee salaries, office supplies, office rent, raw materials, and on and on). So the equation above represents your personal profit. Your income is your revenue. The majority of this money will likely be salary from your day job. But it could also be income from a real estate rental property, income from dividend-paying stocks, or random income you score from your side hustles or weekend jobs. Your expenses are going to be income taxes, rent or mortgage, food, cell phone bill, internet and cable, gas and/or electricity, clothing, commuting costs, entertainment, travel, haircuts, and that gift you bought your nephew for his birthday, among other expenses. This may sound basic, but having a thorough accounting of your expenses is the only way to figure out how much money you actually have.

The goal with this equation is to maximize the "Your Money" part. There is no magic formula for building a bank account with a $1 million or $2 million or $3 million in it. You need to fill the account with money. Yes, it takes time, and it can absolutely be frustrating. There are ways to expedite this process through investing in the stock market and real estate. But you need to consistently keep putting away money into these vehicles. There is no other way to do it—unless you win the lottery or sell your tech start-up for millions of dollars! To maximize the "Your Money" part of the equation, keep your "Income" as high as possible and your "Expenses" as low as possible. Standby for tips on how to do both later on in the book—but first, some more financial plumbing to talk about.

Savings Rate

There's another financial term that is key to achieving financial independence: savings rate. Put simply, this is the percentage of your after-tax income that you save. You may have also heard of the term *disposable income*— that is just a fancy term for after-tax income, which is the money you have remaining after paying income taxes.

INCOME TAXES

In case you weren't aware, the income you make is subject to income taxes. If you are a freelancer, you are responsible for calculating these taxes yourself (or with the help of a tax professional), and you usually have to pay these taxes quarterly. If you are a salaried employee, the taxes are withheld from your paycheck. In the United States, you'll pay federal, state, and sometimes local tax. There are a few states that don't even have a state income tax. Given that some states charge 6 to 9 percent of your income as a tax, living in a state with no income tax could save you that many percentage points from the moment you move to that state. Or if you already live in a state that doesn't charge an income tax, that's all you've ever been used to.

If you have a career that's solely limited to one of the high tax states, like New York or California, that's one thing. But if your career has opportunities nation-wide and you're interested in moving to a state with no income tax, that might be something to look into as just the 6 to 9 percent savings can help you achieve your financial goals a lot faster without sacrificing the the quality of your lifestyle (i.e., cutting down on restaurant visits to save money). If your state doesn't charge an income tax, that's an immediate savings. It's not like you have to lower your housing or clothing costs to makeup that cost.

To calculate your savings rate, simply take the amount of money you save annually and divide that by your after-tax income. So if you have $50,000 per year remaining after income taxes and you spend $40,000 a year on rent, food, clothing, car payments, travel, and all of your other expenses, you are saving $10,000 annually ($50,000 − $40,000). Therefore, your savings rate would be 10,000 divided by 50,000, or 20 percent. Savings rate is expressed as a percentage.

The national savings rate stood at 8.1 percent as of August 2019, according to the US Bureau of Economic Analysis.[2] I bring this up because I think it is important to get a sense of where you stand compared to the national average. For the years I have spent as a financial journalist and personal finance commentator, experts usually advise consumers to save at least 10 percent of their income. Lately, I recall hearing some suggest a higher percentage, like 15 percent. To see the national average so close to that recommended threshold is very admirable. After all, the national savings rate 10 years ago, in August 2009, roughly one year after the worst of the

2008 financial crisis, was only 3 percent, according to the Bureau of Economic Analysis.[3] As you can imagine from being several pages into this book, it's going to be a longer journey to achieve your financial goals with just an 8 or 10 or 15 percent savings rate.

If you are at the national average right now, saving 8 percent of your income, that is high enough that you should be able to retire at age 65, assuming you are currently in your early thirties. Let's say you make $70,000 per year after taxes. If you're saving 8 percent of that amount, that is $5,600 per year. If you are 30 years old and you were to put that $5,600 a year into the stock market earning an average return of 8 percent per year, you would have roughly $1 million by the time you are 65 years old, according to a basic compound interest calculator. This also assumes that you started this journey with no initial savings (i.e., you don't have any net worth, and this is the beginning of your savings journey). One million dollars may not seem like enough to retire on, and it may not be enough in high-cost-of-living states like New York or California or in major international cities like London or Hong Kong, but if you keep your expenses low enough and don't live to be 120 years old, you may be able to get away with retiring with just $1 million!

There are a few problems with the calculation and forecast we just completed. First, it assumes you will only be making $70,000 a year for the next 35 years and that your savings rate will always hold steady at 8 percent. You would like to think that your salary will grow, right? Maybe in 10 or 15 years, you'll be making $100,000 a year or maybe even $150,000 a year. Hey, why not

$200,000 per year or even $300,000 per year? With a higher salary, you'll be able to save more money.

On the flip side, this calculation also assumes that you will always be making at least $70,000 per year and that you'll never lose your job—either to artificial intelligence or some other job-killing threat. Therein lies the problem: it's risky to assume you will always be employed for the next 35 years straight. Anything can happen in that amount of time. If you are a product manager at a start-up, how can you know what your income or salary will be in 35 years or if the company you work for will even be around?

Think about all of the disruption we have seen across so many different industries. A legacy company that has been operating successfully for decades is all of a sudden competing in a significant way with a start-up that has grown at lightning speed and has figured out how to take market share away from the legacy player. It's happening all over the place. The winners of today may not be the winners of tomorrow.

So what if we were to raise your savings rate from 8 percent to, say, 60 percent? Yes, that is a huge increase! You may be wondering how you would ever be able to achieve a 60 percent savings rate. It is not easy. But let's stick with this example in order to illustrate what a savings rate at that level can mean for your financial future. Saving 60 percent of $70,000 per year would amount to $42,000 annually. That's an annual increase of $36,400 from the 8 percent savings rate ($42,000 − $5,600). Again, you must be thinking, *How could I ever live off of just $28,000 per year ($70,000 − $42,000)?* We'll get to that in a moment, but first just look at what raising your savings rate does to your financial situation. If you put that $42,000 a year into the stock market with an average return of 8 percent per year, you should have that $1 million by time you are 44. (assuming that you started with zero savings at age 30). This is all according to a compound interest calculator. There are plenty of them online—do a quick internet search for one to play with the numbers. But, hey, getting to $1 million in 14 years by saving 60 percent of your after-tax income is much faster than the 35 years it may take you if your personal savings rate is just 8 percent. The earlier example is how your parents likely saved for retirement. Put a little bit of money away each month and by the time you're 65, you'll be okay. But your parents didn't have to deal with the threat of artificial intelligence. Plus, it was customary for your parents to stay in one job for 30 years. With the rapid pace of technological change—whether it's due to artificial intelligence or some other change—the notion of staying in one or two jobs for an entire career is a rarity.

A 60 percent saving rate is an extreme retirement savings, and it's a core component of the financial independence movement. That is, choosing to save most of your income rather than follow the traditional "put a little bit away each month" advice that will get you financially independent in 40 years, instead of 14 years.

Now let's take this a step further. What if you were to save 70 percent of the $70,000? That's saving $49,000 per year and living off of $21,000 ($70,000 − $49,000). You should get to roughly $1 million in about 12 years— about two years faster than with the 60 percent savings rate.

How Higher Income Changes the Game

The examples above only dealt with the expense side. In these examples, we dramatically cut spending and increased the savings rate. We didn't consider an increase to the income side. Increasing the income side is not easy. I actually think increasing your income is harder than cutting expenses. Because to increase your income, you need to ask for a raise at your current job, find a new job that pays a higher salary, or take on some side jobs. All of this can take a long time to achieve. On the other hand, reducing your expenses can take minutes. Canceling your streaming music subscription takes a few minutes to do. Deciding to reduce the number of times you eat at restaurants for dinner is a decision that can be made in seconds. Purchasing a cheaper brand of coffee or waiting for the shoes to go on sale instead of buying them at full price are all decisions you have the power and capacity to make in a very short period of time.

Still, let's examine the importance of the income side. Because, at the end of the day, there are only so many expenses you can cut, and it's important not to look at financial independence with a one-sided approach—by just focusing on the expenses side. Increasing your income is a key pillar of attaining financial independence as well.

In the earlier example, you were making $70,000 annually after taxes. Let's say you were able to score a $10,000 after-tax raise. Wow! Maybe you got promoted to a higher position that also resulted in a nice salary bump. Now you're making $80,000 annually. If you were to save 8 percent of that amount (again, that's the national average savings rate in the United States), that amounts to $6,400 per year. Investing this every year over 35 years with an 8 percent savings rate amounts to roughly $1.1 million. That's about $100,000 more than if you had been saving 8 percent annually of your old $70,000 salary. Again, this assumes that your $80,000 level of income remains steady for those entire 35 years.

Now let's increase the savings rate to 60 percent, as we did in the prior example under your old salary: 60 percent of $80,000 is $48,000. If you were to save $48,000 per year with an 8 percent annual return, you'll have roughly $1 million in just 13 years.

For argument's sake, let's do one more example: increase your savings rate to 70 percent. Seventy percent of $80,000 amounts to $56,000. Again, saving this every year with an 8 percent annual return will get you to that roughly $1 million level in a little more than 11 years—a tad faster than when you were saving 70 percent of $70,000.

Both elements of this equation are incredibly important—income and expenses. I don't care if you make $250,000 a year after taxes. If you are spending all of it, you're not going to reach financial independence. Those who are making just $70,000 or $80,000 after taxes but are saving 60 percent of it each year are arguably in better shape than those with much higher incomes who aren't saving anything.

Not to mention, those who have mastered the financial mindset needed to save 60 or 70 percent of their income are arguably in better shape than those that make so much more money but can't muster the mental capacity to raise their savings rate to the 60 percent level. If you're making hundreds of thousands of dollars per year, you may think you are invincible! That you will be making that high salary forever. And, hey, I hope you do!

But just because you make a lot of money doesn't mean you're exempt from saving a lot of money. Just as earning money is a skill, so too is saving money.

The reality is, the more money you make, save, and invest, the faster you should be able to reach your goal of attaining a mountain of assets. If you have more questions about the 8 percent annualized return in each of the examples, see chapter 5, where I cover the ins and outs of investing. Again, the examples above are just examples. There are many other variables at play. If the stock market is less forgiving and you only end up earning 5 or 6 percent annually as a return, it's going to take you longer to get to your $1 million goal. The goal of these examples isn't to account for every variable but to open up your mind a bit and get your thinking aligned with the financial independence movement. Many traditional personal finance books advise saving 10 percent of your income; as you can see by the examples in this chapter, that low savings rate is going to allow you to achieve your goals over many decades. But I'm trying to put you in a position to achieve financial independence much sooner so you can become financially secure before the potential threat of artificial intelligence comes about— when and if it does.

What Is Compound Interest?

The examples just discussed are derived from the notion of compound interest, which is a very powerful concept in personal finance. Compound interest can supercharge your financial goals. Let's say you put $100 into a savings account that pays 1 percent per year. For simplicity, after one year, you should have earned $1 (1 percent of 100 is 1). In year two, you'll have $101 earning 1 percent. That equates to $1.01, which will soon leave you with $102.01. Do you see how you earned interest not just on the original $100, but you also earned interest on the $1 interest payment you received throughout the first year? Do you notice the pattern? This will keep repeating for as long as you save and are earning interest. The notion of compound interest becomes more powerful over time. That is why it is so important to start saving money at a young age—even if it is just a few dollars per month. Because when you're young, you have time on your side, even if you don't have a lot of money.

The earlier examples were based on the goal of saving $1 million. The central question was how to get to $1 million in the least amount of time with a realistic, relatively modest but still respectable 8 percent annual return in the markets. But what if you didn't stop saving after 10 to 15 years? What if you kept going for 35 years? What if you held steady at that extreme savings rate up until the time you reached age 65? This is going to be fun. You won't believe what the numbers show under that scenario.

Let's say you're making $70,000 a year after taxes, and you're saving 60 percent of that amount. Again, that's a savings of $42,000 annually. If you saved this amount every year for up to 35 years with an 8 percent annual return, here's roughly how much money you would have:

- after 10 years: $600,000
- after 20 years: $2 million
- after 30 years: $5 million
- after 35 years: over $7 million

Those are some serious sums of money. Notice the exponential rise in savings as each decade progresses. These scenarios reveal a few takeaways:

1. Compound interest becomes more powerful over time. Throughout all of these years, you are contributing the same amount of money ($42,000 per year) and receiving the same annual return (8 percent). Yet your investment more than doubles between 10 and 20 years and again between 20 and 30 years. Your investment rises by more than $2 million in just five years (between years 30 and 35).

2. Because of the power of time as it pertains to compound interest, you could argue that the financial independence movement is somewhat flawed. This idea that we should save and scrimp and invest for as short of a period as possible so we can quit our day job and pursue our passion clearly leaves a lot of money on the table. In those scenarios, unless your new passion pursuit of a job brings in the same or more income than the job you quit, you're not allowing the time function of compound interest to fully bloom. Think about that for a moment.

3. Remember: the point of saving and scrimping in a short period of time is not so you can quit your 9-to-5 job and start pursuing your passion of lying on the beach all day! The goal is to acknowledge and be prepared for the possible threat of artificial intelligence's effect on your livelihood. Use the next decade wisely to get your finances in tip-top shape to be ready for artificial intelligence's potential job disruption.

Still, keeping that extreme savings rate of 60 percent going for 35 years is not easy. That's why a core component of the financial independence movement is maintaining that extreme savings rate for a relatively short period of time (10 years, for example) and building up the smallest mountain of assets you need to cover your monthly expenses. Because even if artificial intelligence wipes away your job, that doesn't mean you won't have *any* income coming in. Maybe you would be able to take on some side jobs. Or maybe the government would step in and literally pay its citizens with a universal basic income. We just don't know how much money you would be able to make if your job was affected by the threat of artificial intelligence. So this entire exercise of saving almost all your income while you have a job now is really an insurance policy. Because if your mountain of assets can produce enough income to cover all or at least most of your monthly expenses, you don't have to worry as much about what artificial intelligence might do to your job.

As powerful of a concept compound interest is over many decades, the financial independence movement isn't exactly about keeping your job for decades and decades to build up a mountain of assets worth $10 million. If you read the many blogs out there on financial independence, people are not necessarily talking about how to become multimillionaires or billionaires. Instead, they are worried about not having a job in 20 or 30 years because of management restructuring, shifts to overseas manufacturing, and, yes, the threat of artificial intelligence. Therefore, the notion of saving a high percentage of your salary for 35 years may not be practical—but it's still fun to look at the numbers.

Different Types of Financial Independence

Each of the examples above in the Savings Rate section dealt with the goal of reaching $1 million. That was the benchmark I used for financial independence. It may be that your goal is slightly lower or significantly higher than $1 million. Maybe you want to have $2 million, $3 million, or even $5 million in the bank before you claim the "financial independence" victory. There are several ways to determine just how much money you might need in order to be classified as financially independent—both qualitative and quantitative.

Let's take a break from number crunching and talk some philosophy. What are you going to do once you become financially independent? Are you going to quit your job and spend the rest of your life at the beach? Are you going to quit your job and pursue a passion, like working for a local animal shelter or becoming a children's book illustrator? Or are you going to keep your day job and keep working as long as possible—as long as your job remains intact. Let's explore each scenario:

Quit Your Job and Head to the Beach

I'm being facetious in this scenario. Even if you hate your job now and dream of going to the beach every day, be careful what you wish for. You might get bored. While that doesn't mean you'll run back to your old job after you quit, it might mean that you want to pursue something else, in addition to spending lots of time at the beach. According to a 2018 Harris Poll survey by TD Ameritrade, 75 percent of respondents who were financially independent said the notion of financial independence was more critical than the idea of retiring early and leaving the workforce.[4]

Let's say you achieve financial independence by age 45. Are you going to spend the rest of your life lounging around? Probably not. Even if you're replaced by a robot at your job, chances are you'll find something productive to do with your life. This is important. The whole notion of financial independence, at least in this book, is to show you the importance of saving money now, while you have a job, to make your situation as secure as possible. So if you lose your job as a result of artificial intelligence or even something as simple as a routine corporate layoff, you will still be financially okay. That's a different approach than saving up simply to sit on lounge chair.

Quit Your Day Job and Pursue a Passion

Here, you are quitting your 9-to-5 day job to pursue a passion or some sort of part-time job. Maybe you'll be blogging full time and earning money from advertisements or affiliate marketing. Maybe you'll be taking on some freelance writing work from time to time. But you won't be sitting in an air-conditioned office for 40 or even 60 hours per week like you used to. This is a more realistic situation than escaping to the beach. Here, you don't have to worry so much about how much income this passion or part-time job generates, because you already have spent years saving up a mountain of assets that's already producing income. Let's say you were earning $70,000 per year after taxes in your 9-to-5 job. And once you quit, your part-time job or passion only brings in $2,000 per month. That's still a sizeable chunk of change. Because maybe at the time you quit your job, you had already saved up a mountain of assets that was producing $2,000 per month. Now if you add the $2,000 income from your passion project, you have a total of $4,000 coming in once you quit your job. Chances are, that covers your monthly expenses—again, without needing to rely on a 9-to-5 job.

Keep Your Day Job and Keep Working

This is the ideal scenario. The ideal scenario is to keep your day job, even if you dislike it and even if you've already spent years scrimping and saving and building your mountain of assets. This scenario is good for a few reasons:

- If you get fired from your full-time job due to a layoff, you'll be okay because you already have a nest egg that produces enough income to cover your monthly expenses.
- If you lose your career due to artificial intelligence (again, this is different from getting fired or laid off from your job—a career loss is more substantial), you're still okay because you have spent years building this mountain of assets that produces enough income to cover your monthly expenses.
- This scenario also keeps your workforce skills fresh. The risk with the prior scenarios in which you completely quit your job is that should you ever wish to return to the workforce in 2, 5, or 10 years, there may be a large gap on your résumé. You may need to explain to a prospective employer why you left your career and haven't worked in a while. It's difficult to

know how an employer might react to such a large résumé gap. You may also need to explain how the skills you have developed in your passion project (assuming you even took on a passion project once you quit your job) can be useful for the job you are seeking.

- Health-care costs: staying in your job means that you'll still have access to health insurance, assuming your job offered it in the first place. We'll talk more about health-care costs later in this chapter, because it's a wild card in the financial independence movement. A salaried job helps with health-care costs in several ways. First, the access is provided through the employer, i.e., you are part of the employer's plan. Second, many employers pay for part of the monthly insurance premiums. Some employers pay for all of their employee's health-care premiums.

The point of explaining these three scenarios is to show the many flavors of financial independence. Everyone has a different emotional approach to this. Maybe you truly dislike your day job and quitting is a key goal for you. Or maybe you like your job but are worried about the threat of artificial intelligence—so you may stay in your job as long as you can but still take steps along the way to achieve financial independence. Just because you are financially independent doesn't mean you have to quit your job, nor does it mean you have to stop working. As you take steps to build up your mountain of assets while you have a full-time job, it's important to know what your goals are. If you plan to quit your job once you achieve financial independence but also plan on bringing in some sort of income through a passion or part-time job, that changes the equation. You might be able to get away with saving a smaller nest egg of assets than if you were to quit your job and simply live the rest of your life on the beach!

If you plan to keep your job upon reaching financial independence, you may not need to work so quickly to achieve financial independence status because you plan on keeping your main source of income. (Just be mindful of the artificial intelligence threat—just because you have a job, doesn't mean you'll always have a job.)

Be aware that you can be fluid with these goals. You are running the show. You may have always had the goal that once you attained financial independence status, you were going to immediately quit your job. But once you attain this status, or attain a mountain of assets large enough to produce enough income to cover your monthly expenses, you may find that you enjoy your job better because you're no longer necessarily working for the money. In other words, many people view a job as a mechanism to earn money. And it is. But that can also be a pretty exhausting way to think of it. Because the fear of losing your job can result in disastrous consequences if you no longer have enough income coming in to cover your expenses. However, once you have enough money that you don't exactly "need" to work, you may find that the fading of that financial burden may cause you to enjoy your job more. You may continue to work because you want even more discretionary income—income that's not core to your vital expenses like rent and food but money to be used for travel, leisure, or a new car. Alternatively, you may continue to work because you enjoy the camaraderie of your colleagues. Or you may continue to work because you fear you'll be bored just sitting at home.

You can change these goals or toggle back and forth between the different types of financial independence. There are many factors at play here. The main takeaway is: get your financial house in order so you're not clinging to a full-time job because you have to. That doesn't mean your job is bad—it just means that financial self-sufficiency is a noble goal and status.

How Much Money Do You Really Need?

Probably the most important question you can answer for yourself is, *How much money do I need to achieve financial independence?* This number can't be exactly determined from reading this book. It's a personal number and depends on so many factors, including, your life goals, your current age, your current profession and whether or not it is in the crosshairs of the possible artificial intelligence threat, how many children you have and whether or not they plan on attending college. And, of course, will you be expected to be pay for their college education?

The goal here is to get a conversation started about being better equipped financially for the future and to develop a road map for achieving your financial goals.

If you want more one-on-one help with this, it may be worth seeking the advice of a financial professional who can sit down with you and examine your current financial situation and help you articulate the financial goals you're looking to achieve over the next several years.

Here are a few items to consider as you figure out how big your mountain of assets needs to be in order to cover your monthly expenses:

How does your mountain of assets produce income?

Remember the examples earlier in the chapter, when you spent 14 years trying to save $1 million? Let's look at $1 million a little more closely. If you were to put that $1 million in a certificate of deposit (CD) that earns 2 percent annual interest, you would receive roughly $20,000 per year in income (2 percent of $1,000,000 is $20,000). You'll have to pay taxes on that $20,000. If you had $2,000,000 in a certificate of deposit earning 2 percent annually, you would receive something like $40,000 per year in income. This money is completely separate from the original sum you have in the CD—in these examples, either $1 million or $2 million. That's the goal, to not touch that original amount: the principal. The goal is to live off of the interest. That's why your principal—or your mountain of assets— needs to be large enough so that the interest and dividend payments are high enough to give you enough monthly income to pay your bills. The bigger your mountain of assets is, the more interest income you'll score.

What is a Certificate of Deposit?

With a certificate of deposit, you give your money to a bank or financial institution for a certain period of time, say one to five years. In return, the bank gives you a guaranteed interest rate. The interest rate doesn't change during the term of the certificate of deposit, and you can't touch the money in the CD until the term expires, or you may be charged a fee to access the money, which is likely to eat into the income the certificate of deposit is producing. The interest rate on a CD is generally higher for CDs that have a longer duration (a five-year CD likely has a higher interest rate than a one-year CD). The rates on CDs tend to be pretty low, because you're not taking on much risk. It's not like a stock, where the stock may rise in price (that's good) or it may fall in price (that's not good). With a CD, you don't have to really worry about losing the original amount of money you put in. When you buy stock, though, there is risk that you may lose the original amount of money you invested, or at least a good portion of it, if the stock price plummets and never recovers.

If you're considering a CD, you may be better off finding a high-yield savings account. That is, a savings account that pays a high interest rate. The interest rates on savings accounts sometimes rival those of CDs. And with a savings account, you can withdraw your money anytime.

The upshot is that you need to have a big enough principal sum to have higher interest income. How do you get a bigger principal amount? By working in your 9-to-5 job for years, saving 70 percent of your income, and investing that income in higher returning assets like stock index funds or income-producing real estate investments.

How Much Money Will You Withdraw?

In the earlier example, we talked about how to generate $40,000 per year. We determined that a nest egg of $2 million in a certificate of deposit yielding 2 percent annually would accomplish this. But $2 million is a sizeable chunk of change to save. It's going to require a decent salary and a sky-high savings rate that blows past the aforementioned national average. It's doable, but by no means is this an overnight process.

When it comes to having enough money in retirement, there is another line of thinking to be aware of. You could tap into your principal versus solely relying on the interest that the principal generates. If you were to save 25 times your annual expenses, that might be a sizeable chunk of change to cover your annual expenses for a few decades, according to financial experts Cooper Howard and Rob Williams from Charles Schwab.[5] The notion of having a nest egg worth 25 times your annual expenses works in conjunction with a 4 percent withdrawal rate. So if you take your annual expenses of, let's say $50,000 and multiply that by 25, you get $1,250,000. And, of course, 4 percent of $1,250,000 is $50,000. With the guideline, if you withdraw 4 percent of that $1,250,000 nest egg in year one (the assumption is that this $1,250,000 nest egg comprises of half stocks and half bonds), and only raise the withdrawal each year after that by the inflation rate (which usually runs at 2 to 3 percent annually—so you would be raising your withdrawal each year by 2 to 3 percent), you should be able to do this every year for thirty years without running out of money, according to the theory.[6]

What is Inflation?

Let's say you went to the grocery store and spent $50 collectively on a variety of different items including eggs, milk, cereal, fruits, vegetables, and ice cream. A year later, you visit the same grocery store and buy the same items, but the bill comes to $51. It's only a dollar more, right? It's only 2 percent more. But it's still more. That rise is called inflation. It might not be so noticeable at the grocery store, but if you've ever rented an apartment in a major metropolitan city like New York City, chances are that inflation will be a lot more noticeable. The problem with inflation is it gives us less power as a consumer. If the price of goods goes up every year, we better be making more money to keep up with that increase. One of the government's measures of inflation is called the consumer price index, which rose by 1.7 percent year-over-year as of September 2019, according to the Bureau of Labor Statistics.[7] The point is, when figuring out how much money you'll need to achieve financial independence, you need to think about inflation. Because in our example, if you're going to be withdrawing $40,000 annually, if inflation keeps rising, that $40,000 may not get you as far in 10 years.

Again, this is just a framework for how to think about how much you might need to save for retirement. These "rules" help to paint a picture in your mind. Thirty years is not that long of a period of time. It's okay if you're 70 years old and expect to live to be 100. But if you are 40 years old and you have your $1 million savings and you are going to withdraw roughly 4 percent annually from your portfolio, well, you may run out of money after 30 years. If you're 40 years old, chances are you're going to live past age 70, right?

That's why it's so important to make sure you have some sort of income coming in once you achieve financial independence (i.e., and not sit by the beach for the rest of your life). Now, in this book, we continue to acknowledge the possibility of artificial intelligence ruining your job prospects. And that may be the case. Regardless of the circumstances, having a nest egg of assets is better than having no nest egg should you ever be in a situation where artificial intelligence renders your skills and employability obsolete.

Health-Care Costs and Insurance

I would be remiss if I didn't address health insurance and health-care costs. This is perhaps the biggest wild card. It's so difficult to gauge how much you'll spend on health-care costs because you may be healthy now, but how can you ever predict what illness or injuries you might experience several years or decades from now? Health-care costs can be a significant barrier to achieving financial independence. Health-care spending accounts for roughly 18 percent of United States gross domestic product, or $3.6 trillion in 2018, according to the Centers for Medicare & Medicaid Services.[8]

When you visit the doctor, even if you have health insurance, you have to pay a copay and sometimes contribute to the cost of the visit via your deductible.

A deductible on an insurance plan is a minimum amount of money you need to spend out of pocket each year in order for the insurance to kick in. Sometimes, deductibles on health insurance plans are in the thousands. This sounds obvious, but staying healthy can result in fewer doctor visits, which means fewer copays and deductibles. You can't control health-care or prescription drug prices, but you can be committed to a healthy lifestyle. You can vote for politicians who may or may not be able to enact policy to keep costs in check, but that's more of a long-term solution. It's true that you can't control every aspect of your health. Sometimes genetics plays a role or you get into an accident that's of no fault of your own and you're slammed with extra health-care costs. Other times, you do have control—like what you eat and how often you exercise.

If you are going to quit your 9-to-5 job, you may choose to give up your health insurance. And chances are, the health insurance you had with your employer was partly subsidized by your employer. Meaning, the company paid for part or most of the monthly premiums. It's so important to think about how you will pay for your health care prior to making a drastic decision like quitting your job, even if you've achieved financial independence status.

In keeping with the consistency of this book, if artificial intelligence is going to harm employment, that would in theory have a link to health insurance, right? If many people rely on their employer for health insurance and if artificial intelligence wipes out jobs, where will people obtain their health insurance? Here are a few thoughts:

1. Having a nest egg of assets that produces enough income to not just cover your monthly expenses, but also cover whatever monthly health-care costs you'll incur, is a prime way to combat artificial intelligence's possible threat to health-care. Included in the definition of financial independence is the ability to cover health-care costs.

2. Irrespective of artificial intelligence's possible threat to jobs, there is already growing appetite for the government to provide health insurance to its citizens. Just look at the 2020 presidential campaign. There are plenty of candidates proposing a "Medicare for All" plan that would decouple the idea of employer-provided health insurance. That way, if you lose your job, either because of a layoff or because of artificial intelligence, your health care wouldn't necessarily be affected because it would be provided by the government.

Health-care costs are undeniably a major factor in determining how much money you need to save for retirement. Remember, as you get older, you may become more susceptible to illness and require more health care.

Quick Review

Here are a few key items to remember from this chapter:

1. It's difficult to determine how much money you'll need to become financially independent. There really isn't a right answer.

2. Figure out what your goals are with financial independence. Are you planning on keeping your job after you achieve independence? Are you taking the artificial intelligence threat seriously and planning on hanging onto your job as long as you can, even after you've built a nice mountain of income-producing assets?

3. The key to achieving financial independence, short of winning the lottery, is to maintain a very high savings rate (over 50 percent). If this is stressing you out, keep reading, because the next chapter explains how to achieve it.

4. Compound interest is a powerful investing and saving phenomenon that can supercharge your path to financial independence. We'll talk more specifically about investing and the stock market in chapter 5.

How to Prepare for the "Artificial Intelligence Tax"

Have you ever scrutinized your paycheck? It can actually get pretty complicated.

Chances are, it includes the following line items:

Gross salary: _____

Less these deductions:

    Federal Income Tax: _____
    Social Security (FICA):   _____
    Federal Medicare: _____
    State Income Tax: _____

Local Income Tax: _____
401(k) contribution deduction: _____
Health insurance contribution: _____
Dental insurance contribution: _____

Net wages: _____

These are just a few of the possible deductions—everyone's paycheck varies. The specific numbers don't matter. This is just to illustrate that there are many expenses deducted from your paycheck. If you are a full-time employee (i.e., not a freelancer), you'll have taxes deducted from your paycheck. Don't worry, I'm not going to talk about how to file your taxes. Taxes are probably your biggest expense right now—you may be paying as much as 30 percent or more of your income to the government.

And now, I want to add a new tax to your radar. (You're welcome!) It's what I call "The Artificial Intelligence Tax." You're actually going to be paying this tax to yourself. That's right. Think of the amount of money you save each month as a tax paid to yourself. Think of it as another expense—another line item on your paycheck. Don't look at the net wages line (the amount of your paycheck after all taxes, deductions, and 401(k) contributions are accounted for) on your paycheck and think, *Oh, this is great. This is how much money I have to spend on rent, food, and entertainment.*

Instead, take the artificial intelligence tax out of what is left after your actual taxes and deductions and use that remaining amount as what you'll live off of in order to pay for your basic necessities and (some) entertainment. You don't have to physically start making calculations—we'll talk about how to automate the artificial intelligence tax—but this is just a quirky way to frame your thinking around the idea of saving 60 to 70 percent of your income, which is not an easy pill to swallow. Put simply, the artificial intelligence tax is the equivalent to taking 60 percent of your take-home pay and putting it away for the future in case your job is affected by artificial intelligence or any other threat like a routine layoff or your company going out of business.

By the way: getting to a 60 to 70 percent savings rate is by no means an overnight process. It takes time. It requires a lifestyle change.

Tracking Your Expenses

Let's be honest: tracking your expenses can be a pain. There are smartphone apps for this. You can create a spreadsheet. You can write down your expenses every night in a notebook. (Yes, writing longhand still exists!) Or you could put all of your expenditures on a credit card. Shocking, right? Don't most personal finance experts advise against excessive credit card use? Well, yes. Here's a few reasons why:

1. There's a school of thought that says if you're swiping your credit card for things, you may be inclined to spend more money than you have or buy things you don't need. With cash, you're physically removing something from your wallet. That action can give you a better sense of what's required to buy that pair of shoes you don't need. By simply swiping a credit card to pay for the shoes, the impact can be less noticeable.

2. The other reason why financial experts tend to warn against credit card use is because they are worried you're not going to pay off the entire balance every month, resulting in an avalanche of interest expenses. But if you're disciplined and pay off the *entire* credit card balance each month (not just the minimum payment), using your credit card for all purchases can be a helpful expense-tracking mechanism. Each month, you'll have a list of all of your expenditures and a grand total. In fact, some credit card companies have an internal organizer within your online login portal that will categorize your expenses, such as food, entertainment, transportation, etc. It may even categorize it by merchant, so you know how much you spent at the corner grocery store or at your favorite online retailer.

What is a Credit Card's Minimum Payment?

When you view your credit card statement, you'll see a line item that says "minimum payment" and a line item that says "total balance." Chances are the minimum payment is much smaller than the total balance. The minimum payment can be in the neighborhood of $25, even if your total balance is in the hundreds. The minimum payment is just that. It is the minimum amount of money you have to pay to avoid a late fee, which can range from $25 to $35. By only paying the minimum payment, you'll start incurring interest. The interest rates on credit cards can be as high as 25 percent. Think about that! How much are you earning in your savings account? Barely 1 percent? Even in the stock market, you'd be lucky to earn 8 to10 percent in a year as a return. Don't fall for the trap. Don't pay the minimum payment. Pay off the total balance. This will ensure that you won't be charged a late fee or, more importantly, an interest charge. If you can't afford to pay off the total balance, there's a much bigger problem at play: you spent too much and/or you're living paycheck to paycheck. This is understandable, but financial independence is unattainable if you have credit card debt. We'll talk more about debt later on in the book.

The other reason using your credit card for all expenditures is helpful is because it forces you to stick to this idea of expense tracking. If you create a spreadsheet or use an app to track your expenses, maybe you'll have the discipline to do this for a few months, but are you really going to still be playing around with a spreadsheet six months from now? Probably not. With a credit card, expense tracking is automatic: you swipe the card to pay for something and the expense is immediately logged and tallied on your account. When you log in online a day or two before the due date, you have an organized list of all of your expenditures.

Using your credit card to track every expense may not be practical, though. What if your barber shop only accepts cash? Or you paid for a pack of gum with spare change in your wallet? These small cash expenditures are easy to track because they are infrequent. Try to make note of them somewhere—either digitally on your smartphone or in a notebook.

Perhaps the most important outcome of expense tracking is that it allows you to identify trends. Think of yourself in this exercise as a data scientist. Where does your money go each month? Because if you don't track your expenses currently, I guarantee you, you probably have no idea what you spend money on each month. It's very difficult to reduce expenses each month if you don't even know what you are spending money on. You may think you know, but the expense tracking experience will likely be an eye-opener for you.

A few years ago, I was spending roughly $9.75 almost every day for lunch at café near my office. I knew I was spending this money, but hey, what's $9.75? After all, you have to eat! And in major cities like New York, lunch orders can easily cross the $12 or even $15 mark on a daily basis, so in my mind, at $9.75, I was being financially responsible. Wrong!

Here's why: I used my credit card for these purchases—so it's not like I didn't track these expenses. But it wasn't until I started playing with the expense tracking tool within my credit card provider's online portal that I realized what a big financial mistake I was making. You see, the credit card provider has a tool where you can tally up your total expenditures by merchant. As a result, I was able to see that over a certain number of months, I had spent a staggering $900 or so at this one lunch takeout restaurant. I couldn't believe it. How could $9.75 almost every day lead to $900 in spending? It's simple math. But until you see the numbers on paper calculated for you, it can be hard to visualize. After stumbling upon the total spending amount, did I continue eating lunch at this restaurant? No way! I started making lunch at home and bringing it to work. That probably costs $3 to $4 a day instead of $9.75. What a savings!

The point of this story is twofold:

1. Tracking your spending is so important—if I didn't use my credit card for these purchases, I really wouldn't have had a grasp over how much I was spending.

2. It's not enough to just look at your monthly spending. I may have spent $150 to $200 a month at this lunch spot, and, yes, that's a lot of money, but seeing the five-month total of $900 had a much bigger impact on my frame of thinking. So don't just look at the monthly spending; try to look at where you're spending money over several months so you can spot and notice trends. Again, your credit card log-in portal may organize your spending by category and merchant within specific time blocks (such as monthly, year-to-date, and on an annual basis).

Now that we've talked about the importance of tracking your spending, let's dive into some specific money-saving strategies—some you've probably heard of and some that will be new to you.

Save Money on Housing

After taxes, housing is arguably your biggest expense. And for good reason—you have to have a place to live. If you find yourself currently spending what may seem like almost all of your income on housing, you're not alone. But know that a 60 to 70 percent savings rate goal is incredibly difficult to accomplish if a large portion of your paycheck is going to housing expenses.

Here's a statistic for you: the US Department of Housing and Urban Development estimates that 12 million households (comprised of both renters and homeowners) spend over half their yearly pay on housing.[1] That's a pretty frightening statistic. Millions of people, according to this statistic, are spending more than 50 percent on housing—yet the goal in this book is to *save* that amount or even more of your entire take-home pay! Your housing costs can't be this high if you are ever going to attain financial independence. Alternatively, your income needs to dramatically increase, which would, via simple percentage math, cause the percentage of your income that you spend on housing to immediately decrease. But it might be easier and faster to take some steps to decrease your housing costs, rather than try to increase your income. Both would be great, but increasing your income may take longer in that you would have to either ask for a raise at your job or take on some sort of additional part-time work. Here are some ideas for reducing your housing costs:

1. **Find a roommate:** If you have a roommate, chances are you're splitting the rent. And you may also be splitting the utilities and the cable bill, which is another cost saver. Finding a roommate isn't an overnight process, but it may be worth considering if your current living situation allows for such a situation.

2. **Move-in with your significant other:** Obviously, moving in with your significant other is a

sign that your relationship is serious—and that's a good thing! Whether you're splitting the rent with a roommate or a significant other, you're still splitting the rent. That means more money in your pocket and an easier path to the 60 to 70 percent savings rate.

3. **Find a cheaper apartment:** This is pretty simple. Maybe your place just costs too much. Do you really need the stainless-steel appliances and brand-new countertops? Do you need the fancy resident lounge or a gym in your building? Do you need a washer-dryer in your unit? A quick internet search of apartments or homes in your area can give you a sense of where your rent stacks up with other places near you. This information will help educate you on how much you would save if you did give up some of those amenities.

4. **Find a cheaper neighborhood:** Do you live in the most convenient area of town that's across the street from a park and within walking distance from the grocery store? I bring this up because I once lived in an expensive city, but I lived in an up-and-coming area within that city. There were very few grocery stores and the nearest public transportation was a 15-minute walk away from my apartment. But the rent was cheaper and I still got to say I lived in "the city." But the area started to get popular and rents went through the roof. It was then that I decided to move out of the main city to a peripheral city for a much cheaper rent. Be realistic about the neighborhood you live in. You're going to pay for conveniences.

There really isn't any one-size-fits-all approach to personal finance. By no means do I want you to think that the information in this section is tone deaf. If you have children, and you own a home, and you only recently discovered the "financial independence movement," it's going to be difficult to sell your home, move to a less expensive home, and keep your kids in the same school district. However, building a nest egg of assets that produces enough income to cover your monthly expenses is, once again, difficult to achieve if you are spending too much money on housing.

Save Money on Groceries

Stock up when items you *need* are on sale. This might be the most common personal finance cliché, but let's face it: Do you actually practice this? Probably not. This largely applies to staple goods: toothpaste, paper towels, soap, etc. But these items go on sale fairly often. I sometimes see these items for less at a brick-and-mortar store than on online retailers, which are often viewed as having lower prices. So when you see your favorite laundry detergent on sale, stock up! Even if you don't need laundry detergent at that exact time, you will need it in one or two months. Stocking up when items are on sale is arguably the easiest way to make your money work for you without having to make much of an effort.

When determining what brand or size bottle of detergent to buy, you may want to conduct some quick smartphone arithmetic by calculating price per ounce of a bottle of detergent or soap. That may sound extreme, but it only takes seconds to figure out. It helps you determine which size soap bottle is best to buy in terms of price and value. Sometimes a bigger bottle isn't always cheaper. I've run the numbers and there are times when I've selected a medium-size bottle of laundry detergent because the cost per ounce was less than the jumbo size. If you can incorporate this kind of thinking into your spending habits, it won't seem like such a hassle to whip out your smartphone calculator in the cleaning-product aisle of the grocery store.

By the way, the notion of stocking up on items when they go on sale doesn't apply to discretionary items, such as a fifth pair of boots to join your collection of shoes. If you justify that purchase simply because the boots are on sale, you're not doing yourself any financial favors. A $300 pair of boots that is half off will still cost you $150. That said, everyone needs shoes, so if you really need shoes, yes, try to buy them on sale. But here's the key: the *need* for an item should trigger the purchase decision—not the mere fact that an item is on sale. Household staple items are needs. Everyone needs soap and toothpaste, but not everyone needs a new pair of shoes.

The other way to save money on groceries is to rely heavily on the store's weekly sales. Again, this is pretty common financial advice, but it may not be easy to stick to. What's on sale this week can help guide what you buy. So you may be loyal to a certain brand, but achieving a 60 percent savings rate may require elastic loyalty. That is, you should strive to be loyal to what's on sale, not to particular brands. This small change in thinking can help you save money.

Eating at Home

This is pretty self-explanatory, but I'd be remiss if I didn't at least mention it. Cooking at home is usually cheaper than ordering takeout or eating out at a restaurant. That's not to say you can never go out to eat. But if you're spending $15 to $20 on takeout every night, unless you're bringing in a hefty six-figure income, it's going to be difficult to get to that sky-high savings rate.

Then again, cooking at home can be time consuming and inconvenient. You may want to establish a rhythm for cooking at home. Maybe you spend two hours on Sundays preparing a few meals for the rest of the week—whether lunch or dinner. Just eliminating two takeout meals a week is enough to save you thousands of dollars per year. I won't include another example of what a few thousand dollars a year, invested and compounded over two decades, would amount to—but you get the point!

Skip the Morning Latte (Seriously!)

I can't think of personal finance advice more contro-versial than "skip the morning latte." Some people scoff at this. It sounds so silly, doesn't it? Stop buying my $5 latte? Shouldn't I have some morning enjoyment on my way to work? Is saving $5 a day really going to make a difference for my finances over the long-term? Well, let me put it to you this way: the $5 latte isn't doing wonders for your financial independence goals. The fol-lowing compounding example shows the effects that small-ticket expenses can have on your long-term finan-cial future.

Let's say there are 20 work days in a month, so 240 work days a year (20 x 12). If you're spending $5 a day at the coffee shop (and some people may spend more—where are my 2 p.m. coffee lovers?!), that's $1,200 a year. If you were to invest this money every year with an 8 percent annual return, you'd have roughly $17,000 in 10 years and roughly $55,000 in 20 years, thanks to compounding interest. Does the $5 a day seem worth it after seeing those numbers?

The folks who scoff at the idea of "skipping the morning latte" say it's such a small savings that it's not much material in the long-run. And that, instead, people should focus on saving money on big-ticket items like housing. And I agree. Spending as little as possible on big-ticket items is more important, especially if you are hoping to retire by age 65. But remember, this book is about trying to drastically speed up the time it takes to accumulate a nest egg of assets that produces enough income to cover your monthly expenses. We're not trying to achieve this over 40 years; we're trying to do it in a decade or so. That's why focusing on curbing smaller expenditures, like lattes, is important. Every dollar counts.

Store Reward Programs

"Do you have a rewards card?" the cashier asked the person in front of me.

"No," the shopper replied.

I was flabbergasted!

How could you not have a rewards card? And, by the way, at this particular grocery store, the rewards card was particularly valuable because it unlocked lower prices on seemingly hundreds of items in the store. Printed on the price tags of nearly every item in the store was a retail price and then a lower price if you used your rewards card. It was a no-brainer to have this rewards card. It was instant savings. All you had to do is have the card. It took five minutes to apply for the rewards card at the customer service desk.

I'd say you can easily save 10 percent on each grocery order at this particular store because of the rewards card. Yet here was a shopper who didn't have one—and was going to pay full price for all the items when he could have just scored an immediate, say, 10 percent return on his money. Think about discounts and sale prices through an investing lens—as a return on your money.

Now, to be fair, maybe it was this customer's first time shopping at that particular store. The point is, leaving money on the table like this can add up over time and is a big barrier to financial independence. There's no excuse for not using a store's loyalty or rewards card, especially if you are a frequent shopper at the store.

Credit Cards and Rewards Points

My earlier point about putting all purchases on a credit card as an expense-tracking mechanism has another benefit, and it's a direct financial benefit: rewards points. There are many blogs on this topic, and it seems like the credit card companies keep taking steps to "out-reward" their competitors, which is good for you, the consumer.

As you're probably already familiar, there are a host of different rewards-based credit cards. Some allow you to accumulate points to be redeemed at airlines, hotels, or the credit card company's internal store, where you can redeem points for electronics and other items. This is all fine and good. Some of the redemptions have better ratios than others—that is, with some categories you don't need to give up as many points to receive the perk. If you're really interested in this topic, you can become an expert on your card's rewards program. The information is out there—it's just up to you to put in the time to learn the ins and outs of the program.

I also think there's a case to be made for keeping it simple when it comes to rewards. And that means having a simple cash back rewards card. That's right—for every purchase you make using the card, you'll receive a small cash bonus, typically 1 percent of the purchase, but some cards offer 2 percent or 3 percent in some cases. So if you buy a $100 item, you'll get $1 back if it's a 1 percent cash back program or $2 back if it's a 2 percent cash back program. Over time, these cash rewards accumulate. Think of it as a 1 percent discount on everything you spend. Many of the cash back rewards cards allow you to score even deeper cash rewards on certain categories like travel, restaurants, gasoline, or groceries.

You can redeem these cash rewards as a statement credit on your credit card. So if you accumulate $30 a month in cash rewards, you can have $30 removed from your credit card statement. You can also elect to have the credit card issuer write you a check for the $30, but this may take longer.

With the cash back reward, it's an immediate return on investment. You get cash—done. With airlines or hotel points, you actually have to book a trip to use them. If you're booking a trip just to use your rewards points, keep in mind that while the points might take care of the flight or hotel costs, there are still many other expenses associated with a big trip, like transportation to the airport, food, activities, and souvenirs. Plus, you may find with airline miles that you are limited in when you can use the points. For example, you may only be permitted to use the points on certain days of the week. I once used points to book an international flight and almost every flight combination using points had not one but *two* transfers. What should have been a simple flight from the United States to Europe ended up involving the need to stop in two cities before reaching my destination—all for the ability to use points to cover the flight. I'm sorry, but in that case, the points really weren't all that valuable.

Credit Card Rewards Pitfalls

One final point on credit card rewards: it makes absolutely no sense to redeem rewards points or cash back if you're not going to pay off the entire credit card balance each month. Take the cash-back perk. That's a nice 1 to 3 percent return on investment. But it is completely obliterated if you leave a balance on the credit card and start paying a 20 percent interest rate. Again, the benefits of a credit card really kick in when you consistently pay off the entire balance each month.

Credit Card Discounts

When you log in to your credit card portal online, you can view your statement, track your spending, pay your balance, etc. But you may also notice a discount section in the portal as well. These discounts can be at various stores, clothing brands, hotel properties, and coffee shops (and they're well-known national stores and brands, too). These discounts can be as much as 10 percent off any purchase or a $30 statement credit if you use the card at that retailer and spend more than $150. What I've noticed, though, is that it's not enough to just swipe the card at that retailer to score the statement credit. You have to add that specific discount to your card—you have to opt in. And I've also noticed the credit card issuers constantly rotating the list of retailers where purchases can result in statement credits. So it's important to periodically check to see which retailers are offering credits and add them to your account.

Retailer Coupon Codes

This is where you can get a little creative with your money-saving strategies. As a standard operating procedure, before you buy anything online, conduct a quick internet search for promo or coupon codes. Simply type in the name of the retailer and the words "coupon code" into an internet search engine, and there's a strong possibility that you'll discover a money-saving code for your purchase. You can then watch as the code magically knocks 10 percent or 20 percent off your order. It's exciting!

By the way, talk about a return on investment: it probably took you 30 seconds to find the coupon code and you scored an immediate double-digit percentage savings off your online order. If you really want to get creative, try calling the retailer and asking for a coupon code. You never know! This may be a bit more time consuming, but it's worth a try.

Have a High Credit Score

A credit score gauges how well you manage credit—that is, other people's money. Think of it as your financial grade point average. When colleges or law schools or medical schools evaluate applicants, they look at GPA, among other items. GPA gauges how well a student performed in school. A credit score gauges how well one manages finances. A strong credit score is generally any level over 700, but the score typically ranges from 300 to 850.[2] The higher your credit score, the lower the interest rate you'll usually score on a mortgage or car loan. It's that simple.

How do you get a high credit score? You stay out of credit card debt. By staying out of credit card debt—and that means paying off your entire credit card balance each month—you are showing potential creditors that you are responsible with debt and can indeed afford to take on even more debt in the form of a mortgage or car loan.

Remember, any time you're using your credit card, you're essentially taking on debt, albeit short term. That's why each credit card has a credit limit—that's the maximum amount of money you can spend on the card. Remember, when you swipe a credit card to pay for an item, the credit card issuer/bank is financing that transaction, not you.

The other way to keep your credit score elevated is to pay your bills on time. The credit score gets a lot of attention among personal finance experts. It's important, yes, but it's really only important if you are in the market for a loan—that is, a mortgage or a car loan. If you have a low credit score, not only may you be slammed with a higher interest rate on a mortgage, but you may not even be able to get a mortgage. A financial institution may not want to lend money to you if your credit score is below a certain threshold.

Why Interest Rates Matter

Here's why interest rates matter. Let's say you're purchasing a home for $300,000 and you plan to put the standard 20 percent down. That means you'll have to cough up $60,000 (20 percent of $300,000), and the bank will loan you the remaining $240,000 at a 4 percent interest rate. Let's also say, for the purposes of this example, that you're taking out a 30-year fixed mortgage. You're looking at a payment of roughly $1,150 per month. Now if your strong credit score resulted in an interest rate of say 3.5 percent (these are just estimated interest rates—every case is different), your monthly payment would drop by roughly $70 per month. That's a savings of $840 a year. Multiply that by 30 years (the length of the mortgage) and you're looking at a savings of roughly $25,000 over the life of the loan. The point of these examples is to show you that a high credit score matters and that lower interest rates on a mortgage does actually translate into lower monthly payments for you. A credit score is different from a credit report. If your credit score acts like a GPA, a credit report is your college transcript. A credit report lists any outstanding credit card debts you have.

Your Mindset

There is a lot of useful information in this chapter on the steps needed to save 60 to 70 percent of your income.

If you're someone who lives for weekend dinners with friends and spends $18 on a cocktail at a bar every Friday and Saturday night, you may find it difficult to give that up in an effort to move faster down the road to financial independence. It may take time just to grapple with the lifestyle change of saving and scrimping for every dollar.

If you can derive more "happiness" (and I put that in quotes because each of us defines happiness in a different way, but you understand what I mean!) from saving money rather than spending money, this is going to be a much easier exercise. It's about viewing the notion of financial independence as more attractive than buying the latest smartphone or a new winter coat every year. It may be tough to have this mindset on day one of your saving investing journey, but when you watch your nest egg grow from $1,000 to $10,000 to $50,000 to $100,000 to, yes, eventually over $1,000,000, you'll realize that these numbers are more attractive than an expensive pair of shoes that you'll eventually stop wearing.

What to Do Next

This chapter was all about the artificial intelligence tax, which is the money you're going to pay yourself. That tax amounts to 60 to 70 percent of your salary. You accumulate this tax by following the money-saving tips in the chapter and reducing your spending. Maybe you'll increase your income, too!

Assuming you're a full-time employee and you have taxes taken out of your paycheck, here's how you calculate your artificial intelligence tax.

Let's say you get paid twice per month (every two weeks).

First, add up the net pay in the two paychecks you get. This will be your after-tax income for the month, because net pay is the amount you are paid from your job *after* taxes and health insurance expenses are deducted from your paycheck—these items are deducted from a paycheck if you are a full-time salaried employee. But not all of the deductions in the net pay calculation are going to the government or to the health insurance company. Some of it is going to your 401(k). Even though that's money you can't exactly access now (more on this in chapter 6), it's still your money. And you want to include what you're contributing to your 401(k) in the amount of money you're saving each month (i.e., you'll include this sum when you calculate the artificial intelligence tax).

Take the 401(k) contribution (which is a separate line item in your paycheck) and *add it back to each net pay figure*. You should also add to this amount any contribution your employer makes to your 401(k). This number won't likely be listed on your paycheck, but you can easily ask your human resources department or see any employee paperwork you received when you started your job that discusses what percentage of your income your employer contributes to the 401(k). Again, this isn't necessarily money you can access right now, but it should still count toward your artificial intelligence tax!

Next, subtract the following from this amount:

- Your monthly credit card bill (which should have most of your expenses on it, assuming you use the card for all of your expenditures)
- Your rent or mortgage payment (you probably aren't paying your rent or mortgage with your credit card)

- Car payments or other transportation expenses
- Your electric and other utility bills
- Your cable/internet bill
- Any miscellaneous cash expenses you make

The result of these subtractions is what your monthly *savings* should be. Multiply that figure by 12, and that's how much you'll save annually.

Any money that's not already going into your 401(k) or being used on rent or other expenditures is not just going to sit gathering dust. You want to make that money work *for* you. So keep reading to find out how to do that.

Quick Review

A few key items from this chapter:

1. To achieve financial independence, you need a nest egg of money. How do you get that nest egg? You save most of your income.
2. In order to save most of your income, it's important to know what you spend your money on right now. Expense tracking is key.
3. To achieve a savings rate of 60 percent, the big- and small-ticket items are key to focus on. That means saving money on rent (big-ticket item) and skipping the morning latte (small-ticket item).
4. Having a high credit score, a vital component of financial health, can save you money via lower interest rates on a mortgage or car loan.

Debt and Robots Don't Mix

If robots are coming for our jobs, that is a dynamic that will not mix well with debt—whether it's credit card, student loan, or mortgage debt. How can you maintain your debt payments if you lose your job to artificial intelligence? Even if you don't lose your job, what if the pace of technological change lowers the salaries in your industry? And perhaps most important, in the near-term, as you look to build up your mountain of assets, how can you achieve a 60 percent savings rate if you're making high-interest debt payments every month? Wouldn't you be better off banking that money and investing it? Instead of paying someone else a 5 to 20 percent return (this is typically the interest rate range on common types of household debt, including mortgages, student loans, and credit cards), wouldn't *you* like to be earning that kind of return—maybe in the stock or real estate market?

If you have debt, your journey to financial independence may take a longer than if you were starting from a debt-free position. You may not be able to work with that artificial intelligence-induced 10-year time horizon we talked about earlier in the book. But let's put the artificial intelligence angle aside for a moment and just focus on debt: you shouldn't be in debt. Plain and simple. Whether robots pose a threat to the future of work or not, I think we can all agree that debt is harmful to our financial lives. Even if you're not trying to pursue financial independence, debt is not good, unless you're using debt to acquire investments, like real estate investment properties. But that's another story. Here you'll find important information on debt reduction.

Credit Card Debt

For those of you with credit card debt, it's important to know just how widespread this issue is for so many people.

Check out these numbers from a report released in August 2019 by the Consumer Financial Protection Bureau:[1]

- 66 percent of the 255 million US adults have a credit card (as of the end of 2018)
- Total credit card balances: about $900 billion (as of the end of 2018). That's higher than the $792 billion peak reached prior to the 2008 financial crisis.

- Average consumer credit card balance at the end of 2018: $5,700 (this is for a general-purpose credit card). That's the most since mid-2009, which was right after the financial crisis.
- Average annual percentage rate (APR): 20.3 percent (for a general-purpose card as of 2018)

Americans are in more credit card debt as of 2018 than before the 2008 recession. This suggests a few things:

- Americans are feeling so confident about the economy that they are spending on discretionary items so much so that they are getting into debt as a result. They may feel confident that they'll eventually be able to pay off these balances. This hypothesis sounds strange, because if you are confident about your finances, why would you be going into debt? But perhaps you are enjoying life so much that you're spending more than you earn each month, hence the debt.
- On a negative note, Americans still can't seem to make ends meet 10 years after the financial crisis. Maybe they have a job, but maybe it's not paying enough.
- We need more financial education on the dangers of maintaining credit card debt and the importance of living below one's needs.

The analysis above is just speculation. But whether you have $5,000 in credit card debt or $50,000, a key step toward attaining financial independence is crushing this debt to zero. Before getting into debt reduction strategies, let's touch on why debt has a tendency to snowball into much bigger amounts over time.

Credit Card Interest

One of the reasons credit card debt is so expensive is because of interest charges. If you leave a balance on the credit card, interest charges start to accrue. Leaving a balance on a credit card means you did one of two things:

- You completely failed to pay your credit card bill. You just totally missed it. In this case, not only will interest charges accrue until the entire balance is paid off, but you will likely also be charged a late fee, which, as mentioned earlier, can be as much as $35.
- You only paid the minimum payment amount and not the total balance. There is a big difference between the two. The minimum payment, as we discussed earlier, is the amount you need to pay each month to avoid a late payment and, subsequently, a late fee. Paying the minimum payment is better than just skipping a payment altogether. But by only paying the minimum payment, you'll likely start to get slammed with interest charges.

Let's dig deeper into this minimum payment situation. First of all, the minimum payment is "usually calculated as 1 percent of the principal, along with finance charges and fees," according to a report from the Office of the Comptroller of the Currency.[2] Let's say you have $5,000 in credit card debt at a 20 percent interest rate. For simplicity, let's say the minimum payment is just 1 percent of the balance, or $50. According to Bankrate's minimum payment calculator,[3] it will take you more than three decades to pay off this amount and you'll pay over $100,000 in interest charges if you only make the minimum payment. Isn't that ridiculous? How does a $5,000 balance turn into a six-figure amount? The high interest rate (20 percent) plus your $50 monthly minimum payment (that's just $600 per year) doesn't allow you to make even a noticeable dent in your balance. I could go on and on about the minimum payment, but I think you get the point. Here's the pecking order:

1. Pay off the credit card's *entire balance* every month.
2. If you can't do that, pay at least the minimum payment so you avoid a late fee.
3. Aim to pay as much as you can *beyond* the minimum payment each month. Even if it's $10 more than the minimum. That's better than nothing.

More Thoughts on Why Credit Card Interest Is So Harmful

In chapters 5 and 6 I'll discuss investing and the kinds of returns you should expect to see in the stock and real estate market. But let's just say it's difficult to see a 20 percent return on your investment each year in both the stock and real estate market. It's not impossible, but it's difficult. A 20 percent annual return on investment is pretty incredible!

But with credit card debt, you're actually paying 20 percent annually, assuming that's your interest rate (and it may be even higher than 20 percent). Let's say you do find some extra money and you're trying to figure out if you should invest it in the stock market or use it to pay off your credit card debt. Well, you better be buying a really high-flying stock—a stock that returns well over 20 percent a year. Because, think about it, by paying off your credit card debt at a 20 percent interest rate, that's essentially like getting a 20 percent return on your money, right? It doesn't make sense to invest that money in a stock index fund that returns 10 percent a year when you're paying 20 percent in interest charges on your credit card debt.

Credit Cards with Multiple Balances

If you have credit card debt across several different credit cards, there are a few schools of thought on which balance you should pay off first. You could start by throwing the most amount of money you can at the card with the highest interest rate. It would make sense to try to pay off this card the fastest, right? This is the card that is probably costing you the most amount of money. That's because the higher the interest rate, the higher the monthly payments are. There is a direct correlation between interest rates and monthly credit card balances. While you are throwing any extra money you can at this card, you'll still pay the minimum payments on the other cards, because you don't want those cards to become delinquent or buried with late fees. Once the first card is paid off, you can take the money you were paying toward it and apply it to the card with the second-highest interest rate. Once the second card is paid off, you direct all of the prior monies to the card with the third-highest interest rate. Now, hopefully, you don't have more than three credit cards with outstanding credit card balances!

Alternatively, you can begin paying off the credit card with the lowest numerical balance, even if that card happens to have the lowest interest rate. This may help you psychologically, because it'll be easier to pay this one off. There is much brighter light at the end of the tunnel on a credit card with a $1,000 balance than one with a $5,000 balance. The positive feeling of paying off the $1,000 card may inspire you to direct even more money at your other credit card with the $5,000 balance. It may not be the soundest move mathematically, but if it empowers you to tackle your debt, that's great!

Ultimately, as long as you are paying off your credit cards diligently, it doesn't matter that much in the grand scheme of things whether you start paying off the card with the highest interest rate or lowest balance first. Chances are, all of your credit cards have equally high interest rates, so the earlier strategy of starting with the highest rate card might be a moot point. Then again, a card with a $5,000 balance and a 20 percent interest rate is going to cost you more than a card with a $1,000 balance and a 20 percent interest rate. The higher the balance, the higher the interest hit.

Paying off credit card debt is likely a multiyear process for most people. Paying off credit card debt isn't easy. Put simply, the more money you can throw at your credit card balances, the faster you'll become debt-free. The sooner you become debt-free, the more money you'll be able to free up to save and invest and get back on a track toward financial independence. Declining credit card debt balances make it much easier to achieve your golden 60 percent savings rate.

Balance Transfer Cards

I just spent a decent amount of time discussing credit card interest and how it can be a significant barrier to a debt-free life. What if there was a way to slash the interest rate on your credit card to zero? Well, there is.

To do this, you would open up an entirely new credit card—a balance transfer card—and transfer the debt on your old credit card to this new one. This card typically comes with a zero percent promotional interest rate—usually for only 12 or 18 months after you initially open the credit card. But that gives you a nice chunk of time with your credit card balance at a zero percent interest rate. It means your balance won't be increasing during this time, assuming you don't make any new purchases with the card.

By the way, speaking of new purchases, typically with balance transfer cards the zero percent interest rate only applies to the debt amount transferred. If you use the balance transfer card for, let's say, an airline ticket to Europe, a more traditional interest rate will typically apply to that balance if it's not paid off in full by the due date. Then again, if you're in lots of credit card debt, you might want to reconsider that trip to Europe. Just sayin'.

The other thing to keep in mind is that some balance transfer credit cards charge a fee to transfer the debt, and the fee can sometimes be as much as 3 percent of the balance you're transferring to the new card. You may be able to find a balance transfer credit card with no transfer fee. Some simple online research can help you get a sense of the balance transfer card landscape.

Also, not everyone qualifies for a balance transfer card—it's subject to the credit card issuer's approval, just like when you apply for any other credit card.

Student Loans

Student loan debt is arguably a bigger problem than credit card debt. Take a look at the numbers. Student loan debt totaled $1.48 trillion during the second quarter of 2019, according to a report from the Federal Reserve Bank of New York released in August 2019.[4] That is a scary statistic. As you can imagine, achieving a 60 percent savings rate and eventual financial independence is very difficult with student loan debt.

Though just because you have a lot of student loan debt doesn't mean you won't eventually be able to pay it off. If you took on extra debt to attend additional education (think law school or medical school or some sort of graduate school), you may have put yourself in a career or industry that has higher pay than if you didn't have such an advanced degree. According to a report from the Federal Reserve,[5] 22 percent of people with education debt between $10,000 and $24,999 are behind on their debt, as of 2018; for those with a debt balance of at least $100,000, just 16 percent are behind. Hopefully, this stat makes you feel better, especially if you have a six-figure debt load!

It's difficult to cover every area of student loan repayment. It can be more complex than credit card repayment because there are many different types of student loans: government (and there are many types of government loans) and private loans (like from a bank). Each can have unique repayment terms and rules.

Let's be realistic: as much as financial independence involves a 60 percent savings rate (or something about that high or even higher), it also involves basic financial health. Basic financial health means being debt-free. It's hard to achieve financial independence and build a nest egg of assets that can produce income to cover your monthly expenses if your starting point—if your baseline—is negative! And that's what debt is.

Then again, attaining debt-free status is a key accomplishment toward your journey to financial independence. The question to consider is: Can you save a high percentage of your income and pay down your debt at the same time? The answer depends on how serious you are about the goal of financial independence. How much will you sacrifice? We'll do our best to explore this issue throughout this chapter and the rest of the book.

Student Loan Repayment

Okay, enough with the financial philosophy—let's talk about what you need to know about student loan repayment.

When it comes to student loan debt, organization is key. In chapter 3 I discussed the importance of expense tracking and how it's crucial to have a sense of where you spend your money each month. Think about it: How can you save money if you don't even know what you spend it on each month?

Chances are, the bulk of your student loan debt is

from the government. (Do Direct PLUS Loans ring a bell?) But you may also have student loan debt from private financial institutions, like a bank. If I were to ask you the interest rate on each of your student loans, would you know the answer? If I were to ask you how much you owe on each loan, would you know the answer? If you don't know, it's time for a little financial reorganization when it comes to your student loans.

Using a spreadsheet or on a piece a paper, take five minutes to record the main details of each loan you have. These are the important details:

- Name of the issuer (Who owns the loan? Who do you make the monthly payment to?)
- Total balance
- Monthly payment amount
- Interest rate/annual percentage rate (APR)
- Due date of each payment

Next, add up the total amount you owe across each loan. This isn't significant from a financial perspective, but it is from a psychological perspective. You have to know how much debt you're in before you can start to take meaningful steps to pay it off.

Government Student Loans

Let's address government student loans for a moment. There are many different types of government student loans. If you have undergraduate student debt, you may very well have Direct PLUS Loans from the US Department of Education—these are loans parents take out to pay for their kids' education.[6]

If you're a parent with these loans, or if you're reading this and your parents have taken out these loans for you, pay attention: With these loans, and many other government student loan programs, borrowers are automatically enrolled in what's known as the standard repayment plan. Here are the details:[7]

- This is a 10-year plan—that means you'll pay off the loan within 10 years. Because of the relatively tight time period (think about it—it's only 10 years—have you ever heard of a 30-year fixed mortgage? That's a pretty common way people buy a home; they take out a mortgage and plan to pay it over 30 years), your monthly payments may be a little bit steep because there are fewer years to amortize the payments over. The good news is, you'll save extra money over the life of the loan. That's because you are only paying interest for 10 years. Imagine you were in debt for 20 years. That's another 10 years worth of interest expense—it adds up!

If for some reason the payments become too high, you can contact the lender and ask to be switched to the extended repayment plan:[8]

- This is a payment plan of up to 25 years—more than double that of the standard plan.
- It typically results in lower monthly payments, but more money will be spent on interest over the life of the loan.

Now, from a financial perspective, the extended repayment plan may seem like a more expensive option—and it probably is. You'll be paying interest for 25 years instead of the 10 under the standard repayment period. But then again, the monthly payments are typically lower under the extended plan because you're stretching out the repayment timetable over so many more years. Why are lower monthly payments good? Not because it frees up money to spend on another vacation to Europe. No! It frees up money for you to start investing and to start earning a return on your money.

The interest rate on a Direct PLUS Loan stands at 7.08 percent, as of 2019-2020, and that's fixed over the entire period of the loan.[9] A fixed interest rate means it does not change. That rate is low enough that it may make sense to switch to the extended repayment plan to score those lower monthly payments and put the savings from the lower monthly payments into some sort of investment vehicle. If a stock market index fund returns an average of 10 percent each year over the long-term (this is just an example), well, that's better than 7.08 percent. Now again, that 7.08 percent rate won't change, so you have certainty there. Where you don't have certainty is over the stock index fund. There's no guarantee that you'll earn 10 percent every year. Some years you may earn less than 10 percent and some years you may earn more than 10 percent. Again, in order for this to work, you'd have to be consistently invested in this index fund. If you sold some of your shares of the fund too early, the math might not work.

Also, there's something to be said about the power of being debt-free and paying off your loans as soon as possible. So from that angle, it might make sense to plow ahead and get the student loan payment process over with as quickly as possible via the standard repayment plan. But if you find yourself passionate about investing and you want to try to achieve both goals at the same time (paying off your debt and growing your money through investing), it might make sense to examine the interest rates of each option to see what makes the most financial sense. We'll talk more about investing and the stock market in chapter 5.

Employer Contributions

Did you know that some employers are starting to contribute money to employees' student loan debt? Global consulting and advisory firm PwC unveiled a plan a few years ago to pay up to $1,200 a year (for a maximum of six years) toward employee student loan debt.[10] A quick internet search will reveal that other major companies are offering this perk as well.

This is another avenue for loan repayment—it's free money! I bring this up because you may not even know what other financial perks your employer offers beyond the 401(k) retirement plan. It's worth reading the literature you received when you were hired that you probably tossed in a file folder or, worse yet, in the garbage.

It's always worth finding out the perks that companies offer. Especially if you are lucky enough to receive multiple job offers. If the salaries at both jobs are equal but one company offers a student loan repayment program, you may want to consider that opportunity extra carefully. Just knowing that a perk like this exists can help you make better decisions about your career and financial situation.

Mortgage Debt

Mortgage debt is another barrier to financial independence. It totaled some $9.4 trillion as of the second quarter of 2019, according to data from the Federal Reserve Bank of New York.[11] Mortgage debt isn't necessarily a bad thing. If you weren't paying a mortgage, you probably would be paying some sort of rent each month to the owner of a property. And in some areas, it's cheaper to own than to rent, believe it or not. If you're in a major metropolitan city like New York, it may actually be cheaper to rent. That's because in big cities, chances are, you would likely own a condo and not a house. Owning a condo generally means you'll pay monthly maintenance costs to the homeowner's association—and then of course property taxes—which are a reality whether you own a condo or a home. But with renting, you generally don't have to worry about maintenance (the landlord typically takes care of that) nor taxes. We'll cover buying versus renting and how to achieve financial independence through real estate later in chapter 7, but the next couple of pages are going to focus on anyone who already has mortgage debt. Maybe you purchased a home a few years ago and are first discovering the financial independence movement. How do you pay down your mortgage debt? Should you even pay down your mortgage? These are all very important questions that are hard to answer in book form.

When it comes to paying down mortgage debt—just like credit card or student loan debt—feeding the beast is key. That is, the only way to pay down debt is to, well, pay it down! And that requires money. How do you get more money to pay off your debt? Therein lies the key equation of this book:

Income − Expenses = Your Money

So you either have to make more money or cut expenses—all to free up funds to throw toward your mortgage. Making an extra mortgage payment each year—if done every year throughout the life of the loan—can speed up the repayment schedule by several years, thus saving you years worth of interest expenses.

Again, there's something to be said about having the peace of mind that your mortgage is paid off sooner. Once it's paid off, you own the property, and you only have to worry about taxes, maintenance, and insurance. On the flip side, there may be a financial case to be made for not paying off your mortgage so soon. First, you probably can deduct some of the interest expense from your taxes, thus lowering your annual tax bill. Second, it's important to understand what the interest rate on your loan is. If your rate is low, say under 5 percent, it may make sense to keep paying your mortgage and instead of making an extra mortgage payment each year you can put that money in some sort of investment vehicle. As mentioned, if a stock index fund returns 10 percent annually over several decades, that's a nice spread between what you're earning in stocks versus what you're paying on the mortgage. This is known as the opportunity cost. If I do X with my money, what opportunities am I missing out on? If I put extra money toward my mortgage, what financial opportunities am I missing out on?

You may very well have a mortgage rate under 5 percent. In fact, mortgage rates have come down considerably, at least throughout most of 2019. As of this writing, in October 2019, the average rate on a 30-year fixed mortgage stood at 3.69 percent, down over 1 percent from October 2018, according to data from Freddie Mac.[12] So it might make sense to take advantage of these low interest rates and remain in mortgage debt—after all, if the interest rate is this low, it's not costing you *that* much money, right?

Refinance Your Loan to Score a Lower Interest Rate

Another way to take advantage of the recent decline in mortgage rates is to refinance your current loan into a new loan with the lower rate. You would have to run the numbers to see how a lower interest rate would reduce your monthly payment and whether or not it's worth it. With refinancing, you'll likely have to pay one-time closing costs. But the reduction in the monthly mortgage payment could pay for the closing costs in a short period.

Let's say you have a $200,000 30-year fixed-rate mortgage at a 5 percent interest rate. That probably costs you about $1,075 a month in just the principal and interest payment. If you were to refinance the loan to a new loan with a 3.7 percent interest rate, your payment would likely decrease by roughly $150 a month (again these are just estimates). That's a savings of $1,800 a year. Even if you spend a few thousand in closing costs, the lower monthly payment would pay for those closing costs over a year or two. Refinancing your mortgage to lock in a lower interest rate can save you money in interest over the life of the loan, and it can also free up cash for you by lowering your monthly payments. You can then use this cash to either invest or pay down other forms of debt.

Quick Review

The main takeway from this chapter is that debt restricts your ability to maintain a sky-high savings rate of 60 percent. Do what you can to stay out of debt.

1. Know how much debt you owe across all of your different credit cards, mortgage and student loans.
2. Having debt also means paying interest expenses. Take the necessary steps to reduce your interest expense by allocating more money to paying off your debt.

Understanding the Stock Market

Knowing how the stock market works is important. The stock market may sound scary—and it can be! In 2019, an Investopedia[1] survey showed that when asked what negative terms came to mind when describing the stock market, the respondents came up with *risky, intimidating,* and *overwhelming*—and this was a survey among well-off Millennials, those with an average household income of $132,000. Even higher-income Millennials can have fears about investing.

It's totally natural to fear the stock market—after all, what happens if you lose money? I'm not trying to push you to do anything you are not comfortable with, and that includes investing in the stock market. This book is not an advertisement for the stock market. The goal is to provide you with information so you can make your own decisions and weigh the risk/reward ratio. But allowing another day of doubt to keep you from investing can cost you some serious sums of money over the long term. Let's put aside the sky-high 60 percent savings rate that we keep talking about and simply use a more down-to-earth savings rate of 10 percent of your annual income.

Let's say you just graduated college at age 22 and are lucky enough to score a job that pays $50,000 a year. If you save 10 percent of that annually, which is $5,000 per year, and invest it in a mutual fund that returns an 8 percent average rate of return annually, you'll have roughly $1.7 million in 43 years, by the time you've reached age 65, using a basic compound interest calculator (many are available online). And that assumes you'll be saving no more than $5,000 annually for that entire period. (You'd like to think that your salary at age 22 is much less than what you would make at 32 or 42, right?) As your salary increases over time, you should have the ability to save more money per year—even if you keep that 10 percent savings rate stable (but, hopefully, you'll increase it). If in 10 years your salary becomes $100,000 annually, well, 10 percent of $100,000 is $10,000. That's double the 10 percent of your starting salary of $50,000.

Going back to the example of saving $5,000 per year: let's say you wait 10 years to start investing, and at 32 you begin to invest $5,000 per year. At an 8 percent average return, you'll have roughly $700,000 by the time you reach 65. Do you see what just happened? Waiting

10 years to start investing cost you roughly *$1 million!* Yet you still saved the same amount of money ($5,000) annually. By waiting, you end up with about half of what you could have had by age 65 if you just started 10 years earlier at age 22. This is the ultimate example of the importance of *time* in investing. So the next time you find yourself scoffing at the idea of investing because you don't think you have enough money to invest, remember this example. Because in this example, it's not money. It's about time. And when you are young, you may not have a lot of money, but you certainly have time on your side.

Let's dig deeper into the idea of time in investing. With the two examples above—saving at age 22 versus 32—there are similarities and differences. Both examples had the same relatively muted annual contribution of $5,000 per year, yet each scenario had a very different outcome. Why? Because the one with the greater outcome had an extra 10 years on its side.

There are three inputs in these equations: time, money, and return. If you are worried that you won't have a 40-year time horizon to save for retirement because of automation or whatever reason, you're clearly at a disadvantage, right? You don't have as much time to build up a nest egg of assets. Because as we just learned above, time is what fuels this equation thanks to compound interest. So how can you save a meaningful sum for retirement under a shorter time horizon, say, 10 or 15 years instead of 40? You dramatically raise the amount of money you are investing each year. Instead of saving 10 percent of your income, you save something like 60 percent (a.k.a., your sky-high savings rate).

The third input in this equation is return. Yes, if you were able to earn a 30 percent annualized return in the stock market, that would be a game changer. A higher return would allow you to achieve strong results with less money and less time. But if you're savvy enough in the stock market to see returns that high, well, let's just say, you don't need this book!

I understand the initial examples above, which included saving for retirement over a 30- to 40-year period, runs counter to the earlier points in the book. That with the rise of technology and artificial intelligence, you may not have a 30- to 40-year time horizon to save and invest for retirement; you may only have a 10- or 15-year horizon. But I wanted to show this kind of example to reinforce just how powerful time is in investing. At this point, that is a more important concept to grasp than worrying about when or if your job will be taken by a robot! You can't control artificial intelligence's progress. It's not up to you whether your job stays or goes due to automation. You can control how much money you save, how much money you spend, and when you start investing your money. Whether or not to invest your money in the stock market is a decision you can make in the next few minutes.

How Stocks Work

I mentioned the idea of return in the previous section—that if you put your money in a mutual fund, you may receive an 8 percent annual average return. Well, what does that mean? It means the value of the mutual fund rises by 8 percent each year. This is by no means a guarantee, but it's just an arbitrary number we're using for these examples. That 8 percent figure is close to the historical average annual return of the broader stock market, which we'll talk more about in a moment.

Before we go any further, let's go back to basics. You hear the words *stock* and *stock market* thrown around all the time, but in case you're wondering, a stock is simply a share of a company. That's right: you can own a piece of some of your favorite companies, such as Coca-Cola, Apple, or Amazon. Some companies are worth hundreds of billions or even a trillion dollars, so you're probably not going to feel like an "owner" of a company if you buy a few dozen or even a few hundred shares of a public company. To really feel like an owner, you'd probably need to have a multibillion-dollar stake in one of these companies!

Still, by investing, you're making a bet that companies will continue to innovate—that the US economy and world economy will continue to grow. And that companies will keep impressing the world with new products and services that people and businesses will want to buy. And, historically, that has been the case. Take a company like Home Depot, for example. You've probably been to a Home Depot store before. Home Depot's stock was trading around $2-$3 a share in 1990, give or take.[2] Fast-forward 30 years to January 2020, and the stock was trading at about $232 a share.[3] That's roughly an 11,600 percent gain over 30 years. Isn't that amazing?

There are so many other examples like this. And there are also many examples of stocks that did not perform well. What if you get stuck with one of those? That's a possibility. But forget individual stocks for a moment—let's look at the historical performance of the overall stock market. That is widely tracked using the S&P 500, which is a benchmark index.

I took a look at the annual shareholder letter that Berkshire Hathaway CEO Warren Buffett writes. In the letter, they calculate the compounded S&P 500 annual return with dividends to be 9.7 percent from 1965 to 2018.[4] So the S&P 500 returns about 10 percent each year on average, at least since 1965—not bad! That beats what you're earning in your savings account these days.

In the earlier examples about investing over the long term, you may recall we used an 8 percent average return—that's less than the aforementioned 9.7 percent rate. I think it's prudent to use a lower return in your forecasts—better to be safe, right? After all, and this is important, just because the market returned a certain percentage in previous decades doesn't mean it will do so in the coming decades. There is just no way to know what the stock market will do tomorrow, next week, or in 10 years from now. That is one reason why we lowered our estimated rate of return in the examples in this book to 8 percent. This gives us a little bit more wiggle room to account for the possibility of more lackluster stock market returns in the coming decades.

How Stocks Can Make You Money

There are a few ways to make money with a stock. First is price appreciation. This is pretty straightforward. If you buy a stock at $30 a share and sell it 10 years later at $100 a share, well, you earned a profit of $70 per share (100 - 30). If you had 100 shares of this security, that would be a profit of $7,000 (70 x 100 shares). Remember, you only get this profit if you sell the stock. Otherwise, any gain you see in a stock or fund is just on paper—it's an unrealized profit. When you log in to your online brokerage account, it will still show the $7,000 profit, but you can't actually access this money until you sell the security and lock in the profit. After all, stock prices change daily, so the $7,000 profit on Monday could be $6,000 a week later. These paper profits could disappear if the stock price were to suddenly plummet. But long-term investing rarely involves selling stocks. Long-term investing means holding stocks over several decades.

That's why we use a long time horizon in most of the numerical examples in this book. There are plenty of people—some of them very rich—who trade the market on a much shorter time horizon, sometimes minutes, hours, and seconds. They buy a stock at 10 a.m. and a few hours later—or even sooner than that—they sell the stock at a profit. Or sometimes at a loss! The stock market information in this book does not cover trading. There are a ton of books on that if you're interested in learning more about short-term stock trading.

Stocks are volatile by nature. Remember, volatile doesn't mean that the stock always goes down—it just means that the stock price changes a lot and quickly. I encourage you to do a brief internet search on the chart of your favorite stock. You can look at a 1-year chart of the stock or a 10-year chart of the stock. I have a feeling that the 1-year chart looks like a roller coaster ride with a lot of peaks and troughs. I also have a feeling that the 10-year chart looks a lot smoother, and the stock has probably seen some nice gains over the past decade. I have so much more to say about stock market volatility—but keep reading for a deeper discussion on this.

How to Make Money from Stocks: Dividends

The other prominent way to make money in a stock is through dividends. This is essentially when you get paid to own a stock or a fund—whether the price goes up in value or down in value. As long as the company doesn't cut the dividend (which it can do), you get the dividend. How cool is that? Many, many stocks offer dividends. When a company makes a profit, they return that money to the owners. Just like if you owned a pizza shop. If after paying all of your expenses—your rent, the payroll, the tomato sauce and the pizza dough—you were left with $50,000, that would be yours to keep. That's because you are the sole owner of your pizza shop. But with a public company, there are many, many shareholders. So part of that leftover money is distributed to the shareholders via dividends. The pizza example is an extreme oversimplification of all of this, but you get the idea.

Investors of a public company with more shares get more dividends and vice versa. Dividends are paid on a per-share basis. To find out how much of a dividend your stock has, do a quick internet search of the stock's name and the word "dividend." The dividends are usually listed on each company's website within the investor section. Another term Wall Street uses to describe how much a stock returns in dividends is *yield*. When you hear that a stock yields 5 percent each year, that's referring to its dividend.

Take Coca-Cola, for example. According to the dividend page on its website, by buying one share of Coca-Cola stock you'll receive 40 cents every three months or once per quarter.[5] Just imagine if you had 100 shares, 1,000 shares, or 10,000 shares. You get this money regardless of whether or not the stock rises or falls. You literally get paid to own the stock. How cool is that? Now, remember, the company can raise or cut its dividend at any time. Some of the high-growth stocks don't have as high of a dividend because the company would likely rather put that money back into the business to grow the company. A company doesn't have to offer a dividend. But a company may be inclined to offer a dividend because it can make its stock more attractive. Investors want dividends! Who wouldn't want to be paid to own stocks?

Dividends are also calculated on a percentage basis. Generally speaking, a stock that pays a dividend yield of 3 to 5 percent is considered high. Some stocks pay a much higher dividend yield of, say, 7 percent.

Now you may be thinking, *Why not just buy a stock with the highest dividend yield?* Well, if a stock has a higher dividend yield, it gives the company more runway to cut the dividend yield if times get tough. For example: if a stock has a 9 percent yield, and the company experiences a rough year or two for its business, they can cut the dividend by a few percentage points. Also, should the overall economy start to deteriorate or fall into a recession, the company may have no choice but to cut the dividend. The company might need that money instead to keep the lights on.

Plus, as we said before, a stock with a higher dividend yield may not experience as much share price growth. Don't forget the first way to make money in a stock: price appreciation. If you buy a stock at $100 a share and 10 years later the stock is trading at $125 a share, that's not the greatest return over that decade, especially if other stocks are up considerably more during that time period. Stocks that pay a higher dividend yield may be a slower growing, more established company, and so its stock price may not rise as fast over the years. That's one reason why the big technology stocks that you always hear about either pay no dividend or a very small dividend because its stock price is growing fast. They don't pay a dividend largely because they want to put that money back into the business. Ultimately, investors have to decide if you want a slow and steady return, and, if so, maybe a high-yielding stock is for you. Or do you want a high-growth stock that's a little more risky and pays little or no dividends? Again, dividends are not the only way to make money with a stock.

How do you know what is a high dividend and what is a low dividend? Well, we touched on this earlier, let's put a little more meat on the bone in this discussion. We are going to talk about index funds in a moment, but there are funds that you can invest in that track the performance of the S&P 500. One of them is the SPDR S&P 500 Exchange Traded Fund Trust (SPY), and its dividend yield is 1.9 percent as of November 21, 2019.[6] That gives you a sense of the what dividend yield is for the broad benchmark S&P 500. Unless you're an experienced, sophisticated investor, you're probably going to keep your stock investments in broad funds. That means you don't necessarily have to worry about the dividend yields of individual stocks. If you're so interested in investing that you want to invest in individual stocks, this information is more important because you may want to judge a stock's dividend yield in comparison with the broader S&P 500. Again, relativity is a key theme in investing. A stock's dividend yield is just a number. The dividend yield should be compared to another dividend yield before I can decide what to invest my money in.

Many market participants take a stock's dividend very seriously, and for good reason! In fact, going back to Warren Buffett's Berkshire Hathaway for a moment—the company received a whopping $3.8 billion in dividends in 2018, according to the aforementioned annual shareholder letter—and here were its largest holdings at the time:[7]

- American Express
- Apple
- Bank of America
- Coca-Cola
- Wells Fargo

You've heard of these companies before, right? These five companies paid Berkshire Hathaway $2.966 billion in dividends in 2018, almost all of that $3.8 billion total figure.[8] Wow!

One more point on dividends: when you're investing in a stock or a fund, you'll have the option to "reinvest the dividends." Let's say you're set to earn $25 a quarter from Coca-Cola's dividend. Instead of that $25 being added to your brokerage account in the form of cash, you could use that $25 to buy more of Coca-Cola's stock. This can be done automatically if you select on your account "reinvest dividends." Over time, this dividend money will help you accumulate more shares of stock. The more shares you have, the more in dividends you'll eventually earn. Plus, if you have more shares, you'll see a larger benefit from price appreciation. Reinvesting the dividends is essentially like getting free stock. It's this snowball effect that can be very powerful over time.

Now you may be thinking, *Well, why wouldn't I want dividends in the form of cash so that I can fund my next vacation?* Not so fast! Remember, your goal here is to build a mountain of assets that generates income, not a trip to the Caribbean. You need all the help you can get in building that mountain. Obviously, earning more money from your job or side hustle and keeping your expenses low is going to help build this mountain, but reinvesting the dividends is another way to quietly build that mountain of assets without you having to do anything.

Let's say after years of saving, you accumulate a mountain of assets totaling $1 million or $2 million, and you want to live off of the dividend income that this money produces. Only at that point may you consider halting the dividend reinvestment because the dividend income has transitioned into part of how you pay your monthly expenses. But that's a dilemma you would be lucky to have one day. For now, we're focused on building your mountain of assets.

Index Funds

Thus far in the book, I've mentioned stock index funds on several occasions. But what are they? Well, instead of buying individual shares of Apple and Microsoft and Facebook, you can essentially buy the entire stock market when you invest in an index fund. Well, not the entire stock market, but a low-cost fund that tracks the S&P 500, the benchmark stock index.

According to S&P Dow Jones Indices,[9] a division of S&P Global, the company behind the S&P 500 index, the S&P 500 index includes roughly 500 companies and "is widely regarded as the best single gauge of large-cap

U.S. equities." Equities are just an interchangeable phrase for stocks.

Turn on the TV or read a financial newspaper or news website and you'll typically see—very visibly—what the S&P 500 is doing, whether it is up or down on a given day. Because there are so many individual stocks, it can be much easier to look at benchmark indexes like the S&P 500 to understand the health of the overall stock market.

Remember my description of stock market volatility a few pages ago? Well, now that I've explained what the S&P 500 is, I now want to bring your attention to what the index has done over the past 10 years. You are probably familiar with the 2008 financial crisis. You may know someone who lost their house or their job during that time—maybe it was you. Not surprisingly, stocks plummeted during that time. It was a scary time. The federal government had to step in and keep some of the most iconic banks afloat. That was in the fall of 2008. Fast-forward a few months later and on March 9, 2009, the S&P 500 closed the day at roughly 676— a level that hadn't been seen since 1996.[10] It was that bad. Fast-forward again to January 2020—almost 11 years later—and do you know what the S&P 500 is trading at? Just over 3,300![11] That's a gain of—get this— roughly 390%, according to some back-of-the-envelope arithmetic.

The other index is the Dow Jones Industrial Average,[12] which tracks 30 blue-chip US companies, such as Apple, Exxon-Mobil, and Goldman Sachs. There are dozens of funds that track the performance of these indexes. You can invest in these funds.

So when you hear the term *index fund*, it's just referring to a fund that tracks the performance of an index, such as the S&P 500 or the Dow Jones Industrial Average. If the S&P 500 rises 10 percent in one year, and you're invested in a fund that tracks the S&P 500, your fund has also likely risen by roughly 10 percent because its goal is to mimic the performance of the S&P 500.

How do you know if index funds are right for you? Here are some additional characteristics:

1. With index funds, the work is done for you. You don't have to spend hours reading the earnings report of Apple or Facebook to figure out if it makes sense to buy one particular stock over another. You can see for yourself what stocks the fund holds. That information should be available on the fund's website. But again, if you're buying a fund that tracks the S&P 500, you're buying a fund that tracks the S&P 500. And you can't control what specific stocks are in the S&P 500, but it's helpful to remember that the S&P 500 is largely viewed as a benchmark index for the overall stock market.

2. You're diversified with index funds: with a fund that tracks the S&P 500 for example, you have exposure to some 500 different stocks. If some stocks face steep declines, chances are they might be balanced out by other stocks in the fund that face steep gains.

3. The historical performance of these indexes is remarkable. Here's what Warren Buffett wrote in the 2016 Berkshire Hathaway annual shareholder letter:[13] "During the 20th century the

Dow-Jones Industrials advanced from 66 to 11,497, a 17,320 percent capital gain that was materially boosted by steadily increasing dividends." Oh, look, there's another reference to dividends. See how dividends keep coming up in our stock market conversations?

4. The fees for index funds tend to be low—sometimes a fraction of a percent—and some don't charge *any* fee. That saves you money over the long-term because fees eat into your investment returns.

So what does Warren Buffett have to say about index funds? There's a reason we keep including Buffett in our stock market conversation. After all, he's one of the world's richest people, with a net worth of a whopping $83 billion, according to Forbes.[14]

Here's what Buffett recently wrote in the 2016 Berkshire Hathaway annual shareholder letter: "My regular recommendation has been a low-cost S&P 500 index fund."[15]

Don't think of this discussion as an advertisement for index funds. It's merely a summation of what the investing landscape looks like right now—and index funds have been getting lots of attention in the media over the last several decades.

A possible downside to index funds is that investors may miss out on better returns that individual stocks may offer. There are stocks out there—well-known companies—that can sometimes rise 50 to 100 percent in a year. That kind of return is very hard to come by in an entire index fund! But you have to know what you're doing to perform well in individual stocks. Because for every winner you buy, you'll probably buy a loser too. There are plenty of stocks out there that fall 50 to 100 percent in a year. An index fund allows you to achieve the same return as the broader market without having to pick winners and losers.

You May Already Be Invested in Index Funds

I'll cover the 401(k) retirement plan in depth later on, but it's relevant to bring up a common component of 401(k)s: many already invest in some sort of index fund. So you may already be invested in an index fund through your 401(k) and not even know it.

But there is a limit to how much you can contribute to a 401(k), and you may have extra money lying around that needs a home. In that case, it's important to learn about index funds because you may find yourself buying index funds on your own through an online stock brokerage account.

What Determines a Stock Price?

If you've ever looked at a stock chart online during the trading day (which in the United States is weekdays from 9:30 a.m. Eastern to 4 p.m. Eastern), you will notice that stock prices are always changing—every second a stock price can change. The price in the morning can sometimes be much higher or lower or the same than the price at the end of the trading session. Stocks are what we call *liquid*—you can sell your stocks within minutes. With other assets, like real estate, it could take weeks or even months to sell your home—that's what we call *illiq-uid.* The ease at which investors can buy and sell stocks is why the price of a stock moves so often and so quickly. Supply and demand play a role in determining stock prices. There are only a limited number of shares of each stock. So if more people want to buy a certain stock, the price tends to go up and vice versa. What would make someone want to buy a certain stock over another? Well, if the investor thinks one company has better long-term prospects over another company. What does that mean? Every quarter (that's four times per year) a publicly traded company reports financial results. This gives the investing public a window into how the company is doing financially. Earnings reports can answer the following questions for investors:

- **How much profit did the company make?**
- **How much revenue did the company make?**
- **How much did revenue and profit grow year-over-year?** (This is important. Investors want to see growth—just looking at the absolute numbers doesn't tell you much. If a company earned $10 billion in revenue one quarter, that may sound like a lot, and it is, but if the revenue during the same quarter a year ago was $12 billion, investors will likely have a problem with this. That would be a roughly 16.7 percent decline in year-over-year revenue. Investors may start to wonder if the company is facing problems. Why is revenue declining? Are fewer people or companies buying its products or services? Investors want to see year-over-year *growth* in these metrics.)

- How many products did a certain company sell during the quarter?
- What does the company expect to earn over the next year in terms of profit and revenue? (This is formally known as guidance.)
- Did the company raise or lower its dividend?

Earnings reports are available on the company's website and are usually widely written about by journalists at financial media outlets. It may be worth perusing the earnings report of one of your favorite companies. Even if you don't decide to buy individual stocks (perhaps you decide to invest money in index funds instead), it's important to become familiar with these concepts. It may be hard to read and understand these earnings reports at first, but after some experience you should get used to the terminology.

Whether a company reports strong or weak earnings can significantly move a stock price in the short-term. Again, this is not that much of an issue if you are a long-term investor. If a company reports weak earnings, investors probably won't be thinking about that one report 10 years time from now, assuming the company is still around in 10 years! But that weak earnings report can cause the stock to move lower in the hours, days, weeks, and, sometimes, months after the report is issued. Seeing your stock holdings decline during that time can be a tough pill to swallow.

How does Wall Street gauge strong or weak earnings? Well, Wall Street analysts, who typically work for very large and notable investment banks, issue forecasts on how much revenue and profit they think a certain company will earn each quarter. There can be dozens of analysts issuing forecasts of a certain stock. If a company reports earnings and revenue that exceed these forecasts (the forecasts are also widely published in financial media), the stock may become more attractive to more investors and the stock price may rise.

The opposite situation might happen if the company reports earnings that are below what Wall Street is expecting—the stock may decline under this scenario. Even if a company reports a loss (rather than a profit) during a particular quarter, if the loss was less than what Wall Street was expecting, the stock may still rise. You might think that sounds strange. *Why would a stock rise if it didn't make any money in a particular quarter?* But the mere fact that the loss was less than expected could be enough to give the stock a boost. Expectations play an important role on Wall Street and in how investors react.

Earnings reports are released during non-market hours. Sometimes the company will release earnings before the market opens (usually between 6 a.m. to 8 a.m. Eastern) or after the market closes (from, say, 4:05 p.m. to 4:30 p.m. Eastern). The stock will have a chance to react to the report when the market opens. There is also what's known as premarket and after-hours trading—this is a whole other subject that isn't germane to the key pillars of this book, but it's important to know that such a world exists.

Aside from the news release that gives all of the main financial results of a company's quarter, company management will usually hold an earnings conference call with investors, analysts, and reporters. These usually last for roughly one hour, sometimes even longer. On the earnings call, you'll usually hear remarks from top leadership at the company, including, but not limited to:

- **Chief Executive Officer (CEO):** This is arguably the most powerful person at a company—this is the person who is in charge and who makes the major decisions.
- **Chief Financial Officer (CFO):** This person reports to the CEO and makes the major financial decisions for the company.
- **Chief Operating Officer (COO):** This is another executive who can speak on an earnings call. The COO also reports to the CEO and plays a larger role in day-to-day management and strategy of the company.

The comments made by management on an earnings call can have the potential to move stock prices. In fact, it's common for a stock to have a reaction in the premarket or after-hours market upon the initial release of the earnings report. Then, after the conference call wraps up (the conference call usually starts within a few hours after the earnings are released), the stock's reaction may completely change—for better or worse—based on what is said on the earnings call.

For example, a stock may plunge after the earnings are released. But maybe management said something that further explained the results during the call, and the stock erases the earlier loss in premarket trading and actually opens higher once the stock market opens. The conference calls are important. If you own individual stocks, it can be important to listen to these calls. If you own index funds, you're probably not going to spend much time listening in. Regardless, listening to an earnings call or reading a published transcript of the call can be a great way to learn more about the stock market and how the business world works. And, hey, you'll probably learn a thing or two about your favorite companies— even if you don't own that company's stock, you probably use its product or service.

Other Factors That Can Move a Stock Price

Aside from earnings, there are a bunch of other items that can move a stock price, including:

- **Government policy:** The government could pass or repeal a law that may positively or negatively affect a company's business. The stock could react accordingly to this news.
- **Geopolitical issues:** If there is a war or geopolitical conflict, that could increase overall uncertainty and make investors less willing to buy stocks. They may want to buy assets that are less risky, like bonds.
- **Corporate mergers:** Let's say company A buys company B. Usually company A will pay a premium, or a higher price, for company B. If the value of all of the outstanding shares of company B stands at $10 billion, company A may pay $13 billion for company B. That difference (the $3 billion) is called the *premium*. So if you happen to own shares of company B and it gets acquired, your stock may be worth more within seconds after the merger is announced to the public, thanks to that premium.
- **Economic data:** The government and various private companies periodically release various

data points that reveal how the economy is doing. Depending on the strength or weakness of this data, stocks can react accordingly. The stock market is not necessarily the same as the economy, though the two are related. If the economy is growing, that tends to bode well for stocks and vice versa. But let's say the stock market has a really bad month or a bad quarter, that doesn't necessarily mean the economy is in bad shape.

More on Economic Data and Why It Matters

You don't need to have a degree in economics to be informed about financial markets. Here are some of the main economic data points that can sometimes affect an investor's decision on whether or not to buy stocks:

Government's Jobs Report

On the first Friday of each month at 8:30 a.m. Eastern, the Bureau of Labor Statistics releases the monthly jobs report, also known as the monthly nonfarm payrolls report.[16] Because the report is released early in the month, it applies to the month that just wrapped up. In the report, the government releases the number of jobs that were added or lost during the month in the US economy, the unemployment rate, the labor force participation rate, and average hourly earnings, which measure how much money people are making and how much that has grown over the past year.

Think about how important employment is for the economy and subsequently the stock market. If you don't have a job, you probably won't be able to pay your bills and you probably won't be able to go out to eat at a restaurant or take a vacation. (I know this book warns about the downsides of that kind of discretionary spending, but stay with me!) Plus, if you are not employed, chances are you won't be spending much money, and that can have ripple effects throughout the economy. If you're not going to be taking a vacation, well, that could hurt the shares of public companies associated with vacations and travel, such as airline stocks and hotel stocks. That's why the jobs report is widely seen as the most important economic data point—because jobs are so central to the health of the economy and many public companies.

Just like with corporate earnings reports, Wall Street economists issue forecasts on the jobs number. So again, the market tends to interpret the monthly jobs report in relation to how much it exceeded or missed Wall Street's expectations.

Gross Domestic Product

The government also releases a quarterly report on US gross domestic product (GDP). The Bureau of Economic Analysis, the government agency that tabulates GDP, defines it as:[17] "The value of the goods and services produced in the United States is the gross domestic product. The percentage that GDP grew (or shrank) from one period to another is an important way for Americans to gauge how their economy is doing."

When you hear the term *recession*,[18] that means gross domestic product is weakening. Many experts say two back-to-back quarters of declining GDP growth marks a recession, although there is debate about this definition.

That said, recessions are not good. It's difficult to know what the long-term impact of the COVID-19 outbreak will be, but we are beginning to see its effect on the economy. Think back to the recession we had during the 2008 financial crisis. This period was seen as worse than a typical recession. Not all recessions are as bad as the one in 2008. But still, I'm sure you know someone who lost their job during this time. Thankfully, the US economy rebounded significantly in the decade that followed.

Retail Sales

This report is a little less well known, but it is closely watched in financial media. It's a monthly report about how much money consumers spent in the retail and food space, and the US Census Bureau sends questionnaires to some 5,500 entities to gather this data.[19]

One of the key points to watch is the percentage by which retail sales grew or declined month-over-month and year-over-year. The report also categorizes retail sales by industry, such as home and gardening, food services, automotive, gasoline, and clothing. You may have heard that consumer spending makes up the bulk of US GDP. That's why it's so important to see how consumers are spending their money.

More About Stock Reactions

Just because a stock has a certain reaction to an event doesn't mean that it's a "correct" reaction. The market isn't always right. Sometimes it overreacts to things—both to the upside and the downside. Sometimes the pendulum swings too far in both directions. Let's say a company reports strong earnings on Monday morning before the market opens. Once the market opens, the stock surges 5 percent and keeps rising throughout the trading session and ends the day with a total gain of 7 percent. You just made 7 percent in one day. But the following day, the stock may fall by 4 percent, making that initial post-earnings gain only 3 percent (7 percent - 4 percent). It's important to look at the second- and third-day reaction to a stock after it reports earnings. Looking only at the first-day reaction may not tell you the full story.

The Importance of the Federal Reserve

To understand the stock market, it's important to understand the Federal Reserve, also known as the central bank of the United States. Think of it as the bank of the United States. The Federal Reserve has two goals: full employment and price stability.[20]

What does that mean? Well, the Federal Reserve wants to make sure that Americans are employed and that the prices of goods that consumers buy are stable. That is, they want to make sure there isn't too much inflation— or too high of a rate of rising consumer prices. They also want to make sure that prices don't fall too much. This is known as deflation. Think about it: if the price of goods falls, as a consumer, you'll likely wait longer to buy the item, expecting the price to go down the longer you wait. But by waiting, you're not spending money and that can slow the economy. Consumer spending drives economic growth. That may sound counterintuitive to this book, which praises the benefits of not spending in favor of saving 60 percent of your income!

The way the Federal Reserve ensures that people are employed and that prices are stable is by setting interest rates. The interest rate that the Federal Reserve controls is called the Federal funds rate.[21]

Federal Reserve officials meet several times each year to set the Fed funds rate. It's a pretty big event in financial media. There are a lot of financial pundits who spend lots of time pontificating on what the Federal Reserve may or may not do. Will they raise interest rates? Cut interest rates? Or keep rates the same?

If the economy is slowing, the Federal Reserve tends to reduce interest rates. The thinking here is that lower rates will produce economic activity. For instance, if the Federal Reserve cuts interest rates, that should soon lead to lower mortgage rates. Lower mortgage rates reduce the cost of buying a home and make the monthly payments on a mortgage cheaper. This may encourage homebuyers to pull the trigger and buy that home. Think of the economic activity that may follow: you might need furniture; you might buy new appliances; you might get a second car; you might buy some new light fixtures. Not to mention, in a home-buying process, many other third parties get paid, such as the real estate agents, attorneys, mortgage brokers, etc.

Lower interest rates also make it more attractive for companies to borrow money. They may use this money to open a new factory, invest in their business, and maybe even hire more workers. The point is, interest rates have a ripple effect throughout the entire economy.

Low interest rates also have a downside—they can reduce the rates you'll earn in a savings account, which harms savers and retirees looking for safe and guaranteed returns on their cash.

If, however, the economy is growing too fast, the Federal Reserve may raise interest rates to slow the economy down. Federal Reserve policy has a history of moving the stock market. After the 2008 recession, the central bank cut interest rates to roughly zero in an effort to revive the crumbling economy. But it wasn't until December 2015, seven years later, that the Federal Reserve finally started to raise interest rates,[22] in an acknowledgment that the economy had rebounded from the recession.

Throughout the time since the 2008 financial crisis, stocks have risen and the market has become accustomed to low rates. Low rates tend to make stocks more attractive. If your savings account is going to return 0.01 percent in interest, why would you keep your money there? You probably wouldn't. Instead, you might put this money into the stock market in search of a higher return on investment. This dynamic creates extra demand for stocks, which pushes up prices. You may have heard various market pundits over the past few years say that stock prices have been "artificially" pushed up by low interest rates.

Anyway, the stock market tends to applaud low interest rates. If you're going to become a stock market watcher, it's important to understand how the Federal Reserve works and what its goals are.

INTERNATIONAL CENTRAL BANKS

It's not just the US Federal Reserve that matters to the stock market. Although the Federal Reserve is widely seen as the most influential global central bank, there are others that get the attention of financial media. These are:

- European Central Bank (ECB)
- Bank of England (BOE)
- Bank of Japan (BOJ)

Stocks Relative to Bonds

Both the stock and bond markets are very large and complex. This is not a book about either of these topics. There are many books that delve deep into the stock and bond market. But it's important to generally understand the stock and bond markets if you're trying to achieve financial independence.

Since we've spent quite some time talking about the stock market, it's now time we bring in the bond market. A bond is essentially a promise that you'll receive a series of fixed payments for a certain period of time in exchange for spending money upfront for the bond. The amount of the payments is determined by a bond's interest rate, also known as a coupon. Many times you'll see the term *fixed income*. This is interchangeable with bonds. That's really what a bond is—fixed income.

Bonds tend to be less risky than stocks, but also tend to involve lower returns. Traditionally, financial experts usually recommend bonds to older investors who are closer to retirement. That's because there may be less risk involved. And if you're older, you are not just closer to retirement and may need the money soon, but you don't have as much time on your side to recover any losses from the investment. So if you are 60 years old, and most of your portfolio is invested in stocks, and the market faces a downtown for a few years, you may feel inclined to ride out the storm and wait for your investments to recover. But again, you may not be able to wait—you may need the money sooner. However, someone in their twenties or thirties might be able to afford to take on some more risk by investing more in stocks, because even if stocks fall, a younger investor has the time on their side to recover.

Quick Review

In order to build that mountain of assets we keep talking about, it's probably not going to be enough to just *save* the money. That money needs to work *for you*. To that end, investing in the stock market is a popular way to accumulate wealth. Here are a few takeaways from this chapter:

1. Stocks are risky—there's no gurantee they will rise, but historically, the stock market has returned impressive gains.
2. You don't have to invest in individual companies if you don't want to. You can instead invest in index funds that track the broader stock market.

What Artificial Intelligence May Mean for 401(k)s

The nature of this chapter is speculative. We don't know for sure how artificial intelligence will affect not just the future of work, but also society as a whole. So what does artificial intelligence have to do with a 401(k) plan? Well, let's draw the connection by first explaining what a 401(k) is. A 401(k) plan is offered by many employers. Here's how it works: You, the employee, can elect to contribute part of your paycheck to the 401(k). The money is taken out of your paycheck and automatically deposited into your 401(k) account. This money is pretax. That means that your income taxes on your salary will be calculated after your 401(k) contributions are taken out. If you make $100,000 a year and you contribute $15,000 annually to your 401(k), your tax bill will be calculated on the $85,000 (100,000 - 15,000) and not the $100,000. So contributing to your 401(k) lowers your tax bill. Isn't that cool?

You will end up paying taxes on all of this money eventually. You'll pay the taxes in a few decades from now when you withdraw the money—keep in mind you can't withdraw the money before age 59½ without paying a 10 percent penalty in most cases.[1] The money in a 401(k) account is supposed to be used for when you are older and in retirement. It's not meant to finance a vacation to Miami for your 35th birthday. Now, there are certain circumstances where you can take a loan from your 401(k) to avoid the 10 percent penalty, but I'm not going to even get into those details because again, the goal of a 401(k) is to not touch the money until your retirement.

The problem is, if you're in your twenties or thirties now, who knows what income tax rates will be in 30 or 40 years? There is a lot of uncertainty there—just like there is uncertainty on what the workplace will look like in 30 or 40 years due to technology.

Tax revenue is a key part of society. You can't argue with this. As you know, when you work, either for a company or if you own your own business, you must pay income tax. This is probably your largest expense. It may even be larger than your housing costs. This tax revenue helps to fund the government.

If robots result in lower employment and more people are unemployed, these people won't be paying income tax because they don't have income. That would likely suggest less tax revenue for the government, right?

If there is lost tax revenue from artificial intelligence,

will the government raise income tax rates across the board to make up for lost tax revenue? That is, anyone who still has a job may have to pay higher income taxes. That would likely affect your 401(k) withdrawals. If income tax rates rise, whether you are employed or not, those rates apply to your 401(k) withdrawals.

Accounting firm EY raised the issue of tax uncertainty from robots in a July 2019 blog post saying: "If job losses cut into countries' income tax revenues, how would governments fill the gap in their treasuries?"[2]

There is no way to predict what the government may or may not do to make up for possible lost income taxes because fewer people are working as a result of the rise of artificial intelligence. Traditionally, the thinking is, if you withdraw money from the 401(k) in retirement, you probably have low or no income, right? Because you're not working—you're retired. In that sense, you would likely pay a lower tax rate than if you were withdrawing the money at age 40 or 50, when you're probably at or near your "peak earnings," or the highest amount of money you'll earn during your career. But if the government raises income tax rates, you will likely pay more taxes when you withdraw from the 401(k). This chapter is more a function of "food for thought." It's important to at least be aware of the tax uncertainty here.

In the meantime, for 2020, you can contribute a maximum of $19,500 to your 401(k) plan.[3]

Taxing the Robots

While it's hard to predict how the government will respond to any tax issues sparked by artificial intelligence, some well-known business minds have already started talking about this. In a 2017 interview[4] with business news outlet Quartz, Microsoft cofounder Bill Gates brought to light the idea of a tax on the value that robots produce, reasoning that if a worker had previously been paid to produce that same work, the government would tax that worker's salary.

The idea of a robot tax has even gained steam in the 2020 presidential election. New York City Mayor and former presidential candidate Bill de Blasio proposed a robot tax in his presidential campaign, writing the following in a September 2019 news release:[5]

> Corporations that automate procedures which eliminate jobs and fail to provide adequate replacement employment would be required to pay the equivalent of five years' worth of payroll taxes up front for each worker whose job is eliminated.

The revenue from this possible robot tax could be distributed to the very workers it displaced through some sort of universal basic income. But a universal income, something akin to a Social Security check, is a cushion of income given to citizens each month so they're able to pay their basic expenses. This is just one way that the government can play a key role in stemming some or all of any possible negative tax fallout from the rise of automation.

401(k) Employer Matching Program

The other component of a 401(k) is an employer match. That means your employer may match your contribution up to a certain percentage. This is free money. For example, if you contribute 6 percent of your salary to your 401(k), your employer may also contribute up to 6 percent. If you contribute 4 percent, the employer may contribute 4 percent. Understand that by not contributing up to your employer's maximum match, you are leaving free money on the table. Whether or not you want to contribute to the 401(k) beyond your employer's match to meet the $19,500 maximum contribution, that's something you can decide as well. Also, not all employers offer this match—it's a perk! This is something to think about when you're looking for a job or deciding what company to work for next.

One term that you may come across when talking about an employer 401(k) match is *vesting*. Some companies require you to work at the firm for a certain number of years in order to receive 100 percent of the employer's match. Alternatively, some employers will only give you 50 percent of the employer's total match if you stay at the firm for two years and give you 100 percent only after you've worked at the company for three years. The employer sets these thresholds. The goal is to encourage employees to stay at the firm for a certain number of years.

What Money in the 401(k) Is Invested In

Within the 401(k), you can invest in various mutual funds, index funds, or bond funds. You can allocate certain percentages to each fund. For example: 20 percent to a bond fund and 80 percent to a stock fund. Remember, each of these funds likely has management fees. This eats into your return over the long term. Chances are, there is a fund in your 401(k) that tracks the broad S&P

500 index that we talked about in chapter 5—this fund probably also has the lowest management fee. Just be mindful of fees. It's cheaper to pay a management fee of 0.05 percent than a fee of 1 percent.

Speaking of fees, let's refer back to what Warren Buffett has said about fees. It's not something to be taken lightly. You should be aware of what the fees are for each fund you invest in: whether in your 401(k) or in your own brokerage account. Here's what Warren Buffett said in Berkshire Hathaway's 2014 annual shareholder letter:[6]

> Active trading, attempts to "time" market movements, inadequate diversification, the payment of high and unnecessary fees to managers and advisors, and the use of borrowed money can destroy the decent returns that a life-long owner of equities would otherwise enjoy.

The nice component of a 401(k) is that the contributions are automatic—you don't have to do anything. Also, you're not necessarily tempted to sell or exit your holdings when the market declines. Because if you withdraw the money before age 59½, you'll likely pay the 10 percent penalty, along with ordinary income taxes. So the mechanics of the 401(k) incentivize you to keep the money in the market and think long term. That may just be one of the most powerful lessons in investing: thinking long term.

Roth IRA

If the tax uncertainty surrounding the 401(k) scared you—or even if it didn't scare you—there's another retirement savings vehicle that you should know about: the Roth IRA. This is an account that is separate from your employer. You can open it up at a brokerage firm online in a matter of minutes. Here are some of the characteristics of a Roth IRA:[7]

- You can contribute $6,000 per year in 2020 if you are under age 50. If you are over age 50, the threshold rises to $7,000.
- The money you contribute to a Roth IRA is money you've already paid taxes on, unlike a 401(k).
- Generally, when you withdraw this money, the gains are tax-free. Obviously, there are no taxes on the original contributions, because you paid those taxes even before you added the sum to the Roth IRA.

The Roth IRA is a way to grow your investments with a small tax shelter. I say small because you are only allowed to contribute $6,000 to $7,000 annually. With a Roth IRA, you can generally buy stocks, mutual funds, or exchange-traded funds. Even if income tax rates skyrocket in 30 years, you don't have to worry about that with a Roth IRA because you are paying the taxes now.

Quick Review

The goal of this chapter was to shed light on the uncertainty surrounding how society and governments may react to the rise of artificial intelligence—and what that means for your future bottom line. This is extra important because the 401(k) vehicle is a common and widely used tool for people to save for retirement. The success of a 401(k) savings strategy largely depends on what tax rates will be upon withdrawal of the money in a few decades. There's just no way to know. Regardless, here are a few things to remember from this chapter:

1. Money deposited into a 401(k) account is pretax. You pay the taxes after age 59½, when you are able to withdraw the money.
2. Money deposited into these retirement savings vehicles is meant to be used when you are older, during retirement. It's not supposed to be used to finance near-term expenditures.
3. A Roth IRA is another important retirement savings vehicle that can help you save money on taxes over the long term.

Real Estate and Financial Independence

You've probably noticed that throughout this book I draw a connection between two concepts: artificial intelligence and financial independence. In this chapter, I'm going to focus on how real estate is linked to financial independence, and how real estate can build wealth and financial independence—which, obviously, is a hedge against the risk of artificial intelligence wiping out your job!

Housing Costs

Paying for housing is unavoidable. You have to live somewhere, don't you? When I say housing, I don't necessarily mean an actual house. In this chapter, I'm defining *housing costs* as your shelter expenses. Whether you live in a house, apartment, a room—you are going to have to spend some sum of money each month for a place to sleep at night. First, I want to talk about your own housing situation. In this arena, I want to help you decide on whether to rent or buy a place—this is arguably one of the most important questions in personal finance and even real estate. And it's a very difficult question to answer.

Then I want to spend some time talking about real estate as an investment. You could argue that buying a place to live in yourself is an investment—and it might be—and we hear real estate constantly categorized as an investment. But I want to focus on purchasing a home to rent out to tenants to receive monthly cash flow. This is what we would call an income-producing asset: something that pays you every month. That's an investment! And there are plenty of investors who have been able to live on real estate investment income in retirement—and many blogs and books have been written about how to succeed in real estate investing.

Renting vs. Buying

But first, let's cover the roof over your head.

It's very difficult to answer this quintessential personal finance question of buying versus renting because real estate is so personal and local. In some locations, it might make sense to rent and in some markets in might make sense to buy.

When you purchase a home, here are the costs you should expect to pay, assuming you take out a mortgage or a loan to finance the home purchase:

- Monthly mortgage payment (including interest)
- Property taxes
- Homeowner's insurance
- Maintenance costs and repairs
- Water bill
- Utilities (electric, gas, cable, internet)
- Homeowners association (HOA) fees, if applicable

If you rent, here's what you should expect to pay:

- Monthly rent payment
- Utilities (electric, gas, cable, internet—some rents include one or more of these)
- Renter's insurance (if applicable)

Notice how there are far fewer expenses when you rent. That's because only the owner of a property is responsible for paying property taxes. And, usually, the owner is responsible for all of the maintenance. So if the toilet breaks, you, the renter, don't necessarily have to hire a plumber to come and fix the issue.

Now could the landlord pass on some of these costs to you in the rent payment by charging a higher rent? It's possible. But then again, the market determines the rent. If the landlord charges too high of a rent, you have more of an incentive to move out and find a cheaper alternative.

Renting can be volatile. The landlord can raise the rent after your lease expires, although some US states are adding regulations that may make it tougher for a landlord to raise the rent. When you own, assuming your loan has a fixed interest rate, you'll make the same monthly payment for the life of the loan. The certainty with this is nice to have. On the other hand, it is very difficult to "ditch" the mortgage payment should you lose your job and no longer be able to afford the house. You can't just walk away, like you could if you were a renter. When renting a property, if you find yourself in financial hot water and can no longer afford the rent payment, you can negotiate with your landlord to break the lease (you might have to pay an early termination fee). Or you would have to figure out how to pay the landlord for the remainder of the lease term and then move out when the lease expires. Usually, apartment or home leases are either month-to-month, so you can cancel usually with 30 days' notice, or they are for one- or two-year terms. That's still better than an ironclad mortgage. The only way to "ditch" a mortgage is to sell the property. That can take time—sometimes many months—and there are plenty of transaction costs included in that process, such as real estate agent commissions and taxes. When selling your home, you obviously need to make sure you sell the property for a high enough price—ideally more than the outstanding balance of your mortgage. Otherwise, you might still owe money to the lender after selling the house! You can't control the market, so if you find yourself with an urgent need to sell, you may be forced to sell the property at a lower price than you would normally accept if you were not in a rush to sell.

Assuming you don't need to sell your home because of a financial hiccup, let's get back to talking about the financial differences between renting and owning. A mortgage payment, assuming it has a fixed interest rate, gives you certainty in the payment amount each month. The only variables are the property taxes, which can rise over time, and the maintenance costs, which are largely impossible to predict, especially if you live in an older apartment or house. You never know when the dishwasher is going to break or when the hot water heater goes bust and you need to replace it, at a high cost. These kind of maintenance issues come your way at any time and without notice!

With home ownership, you get the benefit of price appreciation, which is obviously not a guarantee, but it's certainly possible. It largely depends on the trajectory of the neighborhood and city that your property is located in. And it's hard to know what your neighborhood will look like over the next few decades. You could also purchase a home that depreciates in value, and if you sell the property you may sell it at a loss. Again, this is especially problematic if you sell the home and the price you receive for the home is less than the outstanding balance of your mortgage. The term for a home in this situation is *underwater*. This was prevalent during the financial crisis of 2008, when home prices plummeted and all of a sudden people were sitting with homes that were worth, say, $300,000 for example, and yet the mortgage on the property totaled $400,000. As a result, it's important to understand that there's no guarantee that buying a home will be a smart investment. Let me say that again: contrary to what you may have been told or read elsewhere, there is no guarantee that buying a home will be a smart investment. Just because you purchase a home does not mean it will be worth more money in 15 or 20 years.

There is also the opportunity cost. That is, the lost money or opportunity that you may suffer by buying a house versus investing that money in a different asset. So if you didn't purchase that $500,000 home 20 years ago, which, by the way, may now be worth only $600,000, what if you had put that money into the stock market, which may have earned 10 percent annually over the past 20 years, for example? That lost return, by not investing in the stock market, is an opportunity cost. You didn't actually lose that money, but you could have made it had you invested differently. Obviously, hindsight is crystal clear. Remember: anytime you make an investment, it is important to think about your alternatives.

Now all of these financial factors may be moot if you are planning to start a family. With that, you may prefer to own a home even if it is not the greatest investment, because you want the stability that may come with home ownership. You may want your kids to grow up in a particular neighborhood and in the same house throughout their childhood, in the same school district, and with the same neighbors. If you're renting, the landlord can raise your rent every year and even kick you out of the residence once your lease expires. The family factor is important and something that is hard for this book or any book to get in the way of. If you're expecting a final answer from this chapter as to whether you should rent or buy, you're not going to get one. It's a personal decision based on many factors. But this chapter aims to lay out information you need to make an informed decision on how to proceed.

Sunk Costs of Home Ownership

As briefly discussed earlier, when you purchase a home, there are a few unavoidable transaction costs. In business, they're called "sunk costs." It's money you're never going to get back—the cost of doing business. Here are the main ones:

- **Closing costs:** These can be as high as a few percentage points of the total purchase price of the property. So if you are buying a $300,000 home, you may pay around $10,000 in closing costs.
- **Real estate agent commission:** This only applies if you hire a real estate agent to sell and list your home—they usually charge a commission of 3 to 5 percent of the price the home sells for. You could list and sell your home yourself ("for sale by owner"), but this is pretty time consuming. You may have to hold open houses every weekend, where prospective buyers are free to enter your home to tour the property. If you hired a real estate agent, they would handle this for you. Real estate agents also handle all of the marketing of the home: taking professional photos of the interior and exterior, listing the home on different real estate websites, etc.
- **Legal fees:** This may or may not be included in your closing cost estimate, but with the sale or purchase of a property, there are many documents involved and you may have to hire an attorney to guide you through this process.
- **Home inspection fees:** Whether you buy a home for yourself or if you are buying an investment property to rent out to tenants, chances are you will choose to have the home inspected by a home inspector to make sure it's

structurally sound. This can cost several hundred dollars—and if the inspector finds too many problems with the house and you decide to not go ahead with the purchase, well, you just spent hundreds of dollars on an inspection for a home that you're not even going to buy. You would have to eat that cost and continue your home search.

Not having a home inspector review your home is risky—what if you're purchasing a home that has a faulty foundation, and you end up discovering this years later? Now you're slammed with a big expense. If your home inspector uncovers these issues before you make the purchase, you can either back out of the deal or ask the seller for a credit off the purchase price to help you pay for some of the repairs.

Given all of these sunk costs, when purchasing a home, you generally should plan on staying in the home for at least several years. If you buy a home and then wish to sell it in a year, you may not achieve enough price appreciation in that year to cover the aforementioned transaction costs.

Mortgage Interest

Let's talk more mechanically about arguably the biggest cost associated with purchasing a home: the mortgage and the accompanying interest you will pay as a result of borrowing this money. By the way, a mortgage is just another term for a loan. With a mortgage, a bank or financial institution is giving you the money to purchase the home now. In exchange, you'll pay back that loan in small pieces each month—plus interest—over several years. This is how the bank or financial institution makes its money. The cost to borrow the money called *interest*. You pay this cost. This cost is determined by the interest rate attached to the loan.

The interest rate you pay on a mortgage matters for your finances. And the one part of the interest rate calculation that you can control is your credit history. If you have credit card debt and a history of paying bills late, you will likely have a lower credit score and with that, the lender could charge you a higher interest rate as a result. With a low credit score, you are viewed as a riskier borrower in the eyes of the lender. The lender would be worried that you may not pay back the loan in the future or that you may make late payments, given your past financial struggles. As such, the lender will likely charge you a higher interest rate—this is essentially an extra cash cushion for the bank because they are taking on more risk by lending to you.

If you are in the market for a mortgage, take steps to increase your credit score (see page 72 for a discussion of these strategies) so you can lock in a lower interest rate and score lower monthly mortgage payments.

The Numbers Behind Mortgage Interest

Let's say you are buying a $500,000 home and you plan to put 20 percent down, or $100,000, and borrow the rest. That means your mortgage would be for $400,000. Let's also say you're going to take out a 30-year fixed-rate mortgage with a rate at 3.75 percent. That means your interest rate would stay the same for 30 years and you would have 30 years to pay off the loan of $400,000 plus the interest. Well, how much is the interest over that 30 year period? Over $260,000! So that $500,000 house really cost you $660,000. Not to mention 30 years' worth of annual property taxes and maintenance. If you own a home for 30 years, chances are you're going to need a new roof and new appliances eventually. You may also need new windows, a new furnace, a new hot water heater, and several new paint jobs. So by buying this home, you're banking on getting some nice price appreciation over that 30-year period to cover all of these costs. And again, like the stock market, price appreciation is only realized when you sell the asset. Therefore, if you buy a home for $500,000 and in 30 years it's worth $1,500,000, you will only receive this $1,500,000 if you sell the property.

So if you take the $260,000 in total interest payments, which again is paid over 30 years, and divide it by 30, you see that you'll pay roughly $8,700 per year in interest. On a $500,000 house, let's say your property taxes are $10,000 annually. (I'm just going to assume property taxes stay the same throughout the 30-year term—this isn't realistic, but it just makes the math in this example much easier to understand.) And let's say you're paying 1 percent of the purchase price annually in maintenance of the property, which turns out to be $5,000 per year. Per year, you're spending $23,700 on interest, property taxes, and maintenance. This figure doesn't even include the principal of your mortgage (remember: with a mortgage, you're paying the monthly payment for the actual loan amount *and* the interest—no bank is just going to give you free money; they're going to charge you fees for the privilege of receiving that loan).

If you were to put that $23,700 in the stock market, earning 8 percent annually, you would have roughly $2.6 million at the end of that 30-year period. Could your home's value surge to $2.6 million at the end of 30 years? It's possible. But it does seem unlikely: to go from a $500,000 purchase price to a $2.6 million sales price over 30 years. Now, if you were to take that $2.6 million at the end of the 30-year period and cash it out of the stock market and instead invest it into a safer asset like bonds—or even a high-yield savings account or a certificate of deposit—at a 2 percent average annual return—that would give you roughly $50,000 annually in interest income. Not bad, right? That's a little over $4,000 per month. I don't care what city you live in—$4,000 in monthly interest income can give you a pretty nice life, especially if you combine it with income from a job.

Now this is a hypothetical example. As we talked about earlier, we have no idea what the stock market will do in the next day or the next 30 years. Nor do we know by how much home prices will rise over the next year or even 30 years.

Let's look at this example a little more holistically. Your total monthly mortgage payment to the bank over this 30-year period would be roughly $1,850—that includes the principal and interest. Now, if your property taxes are $10,000 annually and the maintenance costs are $5,000 annually, that's $15,000 annually, or $1,250 monthly. The $1,850 mortgage payment plus the taxes and maintenance equals an expenditure of $3,100 per month. That's your total monthly cost for owning this home. By the way, this does not include home insurance. But let's put that aside for a moment, because if you rent a house or apartment, you may end up getting renter's insurance. What can you get for $3,100 in rent in your neighborhood—the same size house? If you can get the same house for $2,100 as a rental, it might make more sense to rent. That's because you don't have to come up with a $100,000 down payment (remember 20 percent of $500,000 is $100,000), and you won't have to worry about property taxes and maintenance and interest on a loan. Now, yes your rent could rise sharply over time. But again, if you are truly interested in putting each dollar of your net worth to work, you would probably put that money you would have spent on the down payment for the house into the stock market. Eventually that money is likely to yield monthly dividend payments to help you cover the cost of your rent.

For more context, I had the opportunity to interview Robert J. Shiller, Sterling Professor of Economics at Yale University, a 2013 Nobel laureate in economics, and the author of many books, including *Narrative Economics: How Stories Go Viral and Drive Major Economic Events*. He told me that there is a good chance that the long-term historical returns for homes, adjusted for maintenance costs, are negative.[1]

I've heard several financial experts say that renting is like throwing money down the drain each month. But Professor Shiller disagrees:

> When you're renting, you put the money into another investment—if it's the stock market, it has had historically higher returns and if you want to, you can leverage that up. Instead of borrowing to buy a house, you borrow to buy stock. That gets risky. I'm not suggesting that most people should do that.[2]

Professor Shiller's point is that if you were to rent instead of taking out a mortgage to buy a home, you would not need to come up with such a large down payment. That money, instead, would go into another asset class, such as the stock market.

Remember when we talked about the amount of money in interest you would pay on a 30-year fixed-rate mortgage earlier? Well, Professor Shiller likens that interest to rent. Thinking of the equation in these terms can help you understand why renting isn't like throwing money down the drain. When you purchase a home, the interest part of your mortgage payment is nonreturnable. With the principal part, that money is going toward you actually owning the home outright one day, which is good. But the interest is just a cost of doing business.

Owning a Home Outright

There is something to be said about the notion of owning a home outright. If you purchase a property and stay in it for a few decades, you may have the opportunity to pay off the entire loan completely. If you take out a 30-year fixed-rate mortgage, at the end of the 30-year period, you will no longer have a mortgage payment. You will truly own the house. You will only be responsible for the taxes, maintenance, and insurance. By purchasing a home, you have a chance to one day have very low housing expenses, because you'll eventually own your property outright.

The only problem with this is the opportunity cost from all of these extra expenses in owning a home. For example, if you were to rent and invest the sum of a down payment, property taxes, loan interest, and maintenance costs into the stock market, in 30 years you would likely have a mountain of assets that produces enough interest to cover your rent. Get it? Per the example a few pages back, putting the annual interest, taxes, and maintenance cost into the stock market over 30 years led to a $2.6 million figure, thanks to compound interest. Just putting $2.6 million in a certificate of deposit, which is a very safe investment, earning 2 percent annually, for example, would likely give you enough income to rent a house or an apartment. Renting can make a lot of sense if you are smart about what you do with the rest of your money. As is the case with almost everything in finance, you can't look at anything in a vacuum. It's all relative. If I'm going to do X with my money, what am I missing out on? It's all about the opportunity cost. Don't be surprised to see this concept come up continuously in your study of finance and financial independence.

If you're going to rent for the rest of your life and not invest in any other asset class and just spend your money on expensive smartphones, vacations, and clothing—well, you're not exactly setting yourself up for a successful financial future.

This all is an extremely complex and personal issue that cannot be answered by a financial expert. But the issue of housing costs is a significant component of your quest to become financially independent because, chances are, housing is your second largest expense after taxes. Plus, purchasing property can be a key component of your overall net worth, especially if you are lucky enough to buy a property inexpensively and sell it at a significant profit years later.

Rental Properties

I want to shift gears and talk about real estate as an investment. Yes, you could argue that buying a home for you to live in is an investment. But, as discussed, you are paying a lot of expenses when you buy a home, and you're not exactly getting anything paid back to you each month, right? Where is your monthly check made out to *you*? All you're doing is paying others: the bank, the city for taxes, the insurance company, and the landscaper. If you're lucky, you can sell your home for a profit in 5, 10, or 30 years. But your home isn't paying you each month in cash.

A true investment property is something that provides monthly cash flow for you. Just like when you purchase a stock, it may have a dividend—that's cash flow. That is cash coming into your wallet. If you buy a house and it costs $1,000 per month, but you can rent it out to a tenant for $1,300 a month, you're profiting $300. That is cash coming into your wallet. See the difference?

There are many blogs and books about real estate investing. In my opinion, some of these publications make investing in real estate look too easy. That's not to say that you can't find nice real estate investment opportunities, but it's complicated, and there are a lot of moving parts to keep track of. It requires work, time, and effort: something you may not have if you already have a busy day job. But I hope that the next several pages at least open your mind up to this possibility as a way to invest your money and develop some additional income streams beyond just your 9-to-5 job that may or may not be around in 10 to 20 years due to the rise of artificial intelligence.

Live in One Unit and Rent Out the Other

Before I delve into the details of becoming a real estate investor, let's pause for a moment and talk about a hybrid real estate strategy. This combines purchasing a home for you to live in, and renting part of it to tenants to help cover your monthly expenses. This is the "live for free" strategy, which is key to achieving financial independence. I mentioned earlier that housing costs are probably your biggest expenses after taxes. Well, what if you could dramatically reduce your own housing costs to either nothing or a paltry sum each month?

Here's how this hybrid strategy works: buy a two-unit house; you live in one unit and rent out the other unit to a tenant. Chances are, the rent from the tenant will cover most, if not all, of your monthly expenses for the entire two-unit property, including the mortgage payment, taxes, insurance, and maintenance. You may even find yourself making a little bit of a profit. But the goal in this case is not necessarily trying to make a profit. It's simply covering your monthly expenses for the entire property. The goal is to break even so you personally can live for free. Instead, you essentially would have the tenant paying your housing costs. How cool is that? Why doesn't everyone do this? Well, that's a good question.

Owning a two-unit house and renting out one unit can be an effective wealth-building strategy. If your tenant is paying your housing costs, think about what you could do with the money you save. You could invest it into other assets, like the stock market, to further boost your path to financial independence.

Here are the benefits to this strategy:

- **Tenant pays your mortgage:** By buying a two- or three-unit building and living in one unit and renting out the remaining units, you put yourself in a position to have free or almost free housing. Even if you're still paying $200 to $300 a month for all the home's expenses after receiving the rent from your tenant, that's still an incredibly low price to pay for housing. If you're lucky, you might even find yourself making a little profit too.
- **Interest rates:** If you purchase a two- or three-unit building and you live in one of the units, that is still considered your primary residence. That means you should be able to gain access to the residential interest rates, which are lower than interest rates on investment property loans. Investment property loans are for home purchases where you will *not* be living on the property. Talk to your lender about this difference. It's an important difference. Interest rates tend to be higher on investment properties because the bank generally views this situation as riskier for them. If you are not living on the property, they may worry that there is increased risk of something bad happening to the property. For instance, if you live on the property, you have more incentive to maintain it and take care of it, because, well, you live there!
- **Keeping an eye on your property:** Because you live on the premises, you may not need to

hire a property manager, as you might if you were purchasing a two- or three-family building as an investment property and not living in one of the units. A property manager may charge as much as 10 percent of the total monthly rent to manage the property. This can quickly eat into your cash flow. Since you'll be on-site, it is easier for you to manage the property yourself and collect the rent yourself from the tenants. I didn't say managing the property will be easy—just easier than if you were managing it yourself and you lived off-site. Also, there are plenty of software programs online that allow tenants to pay their rent electronically. So when I say "collect the rent," I don't exactly mean you knocking on their door asking for the rent each month.

Here are the downsides this strategy:

- **Managing a property can be challenging:** You just worked a 10-hour day at your full-time job and at 8 p.m., your tenant knocks on your door or texts you complaining of a broken toilet. You now have to fix it yourself or call a plumber to do so, which will cost money. You're also probably very tired after working a 10-hour day, and you're probably not interested in fielding complaints from your tenants. But this kind of stuff is par for the course if you are going to manage a property yourself.
- **Maintenance costs:** The bigger the property you purchase, the more maintenance costs it will have. If you buy a two- or three-unit

property, you're going to have two or three kitchens and multiple bathrooms. That means there's a greater risk that a refrigerator breaks or a furnace needs to be replaced for a cost of several thousand dollars. While the rent from this larger multifamily property is likely covering your own individual housing costs, an unexpected repair from one of the tenant's units could eat into your returns. Again, it is very difficult to predict future maintenance costs of a property, especially if it is an older property.

- **Tenants may stop paying rent:** There is always a risk that your tenant stops paying rent for whatever reason. Maybe they are going through a financial hardship or maybe they just don't feel like paying rent. Regardless of the reason, if you don't have that revenue coming in, you're going to have to foot the bill for the mortgage of the entire building by yourself. A two-unit building likely costs more money than if you had purchased a single-family house for just you to live in. You may not be able to afford the mortgage on this two-family unit without the revenue coming in from the tenant. Plus, if a tenant does not pay, you may have to start an eviction process, which likely involves hiring an attorney. That can be expensive, time consuming, and stressful.

- **Selling your property:** Selling a multifamily residence can be tougher than a single-family home. This is because you're likely catering to an investor audience. Anyone who is looking for a single-family property (i.e., they don't want to be a landlord), probably won't even consider buying your property, which would require dealing with tenants. So it may take you longer to find a buyer if you eventually decide to move out and sell your property.

- **Liability:** If your tenant trips on the steps leading up to the building because you didn't shovel the snow properly, and they are injured, they could sue you for damages. Consider purchasing some sort of landlord liability insurance policy on the house to help you in a situation like this. But the risk of getting sued is still a scary thought.

- **Difficulty in finding a two-unit building:** Finding a two- or three-unit building where you can live in one of the units and rent out the others can be challenging. Some neighborhoods have mostly single-family residences. The multifamily ones may be in less desirable locations. It's not that common for a random two-unit property to be situated in a sea of single-family homes. If you're interested in this hybrid strategy, you may have to be flexible on the location. Investing in two- or three-unit properties may not be a possibility in your area. This strategy isn't for everyone!

Buying an Investment Property

Buying an investment property to rent out to tenants is another way to generate cash flow each month. In this situation, you would *not* live on the property. It would solely exist for your tenants. Remember how we were talking earlier about how nice it would be to have a mountain of assets that produces enough income to cover your monthly expenses? So far, our conclusion was that a good baseline is having at least $1 million sitting in a certificate of deposit earning about 2 percent annually. That would provide roughly $20,000 per year, which is about $1,700 per month. Chances are that is not enough to cover your monthly expenses completely, but that income plus some sort of a part-time job or side hustle may be enough. Obviously, it takes time to save up $1 million or $2 million or whatever your goal is. As explained, it can take well over a decade and require some significant sacrifices, like saving as much as 60 percent of your take home pay and curtailing your spending in almost every area of your budget.

Now what if you could earn that $1,700 per month (the amount you would receive in interest if you have $1 million sitting in a certificate of deposit earning 2 percent) without having to save $1 million? What if you could purchase a series of real estate properties that brings in that kind of cash flow each month? And you would take out mortgages on these properties that would require a down payment of only 25 percent of the purchase price. Meaning, you are personally shelling out 25 percent of the purchase price to own a property that gives you some sizeable income each month. Well, you can do this. It's not easy. But it can be done.

What I'm talking about here is buying a single-family house or a small apartment building (say one to four units) solely as an investment. You would not be living there at all. The hope is that the tenant's rent would cover the mortgage, taxes, insurance, maintenance, and utilities, *and* leave you a profit each month. There are people who have multiple rental properties that they acquire over time and each produces a certain amount of cash flow. Collectively, across all of their different rental properties, this may be enough money for them to live off of and then some!

Rental properties are what we call income-producing assets—just like certain stocks pay dividends, which we covered extensively earlier in the book. These are assets that you purchase—but they pay you just for owning them. Forget about the price appreciation that may or may not come once you sell the asset. Right now, the discussion is about the income-producing component of an asset. Do you see the difference? With real estate investing, I'm not necessarily buying an investment property for $300,000 hoping that it will be worth $700,000 in 15 years. That kind of appreciation would be great. But in this situation, my goal of buying an investment property is for the monthly positive cash flow. That is, cash coming into your wallet every month. Profits, dividends, cash flow—whatever you want to call it. I want to get paid every month for owning this property.

How to Value a Property

Finding the right property to invest in isn't easy. Doing a quick internet search of available properties in your neighborhood may not be enough. I've heard stories of real estate investors literally sending letters to homeowners asking if they would like to sell their homes. These letters are sent to homes that are not even listed for sale. The thinking is that you might be able to score a better deal on an off-market property.

You may also try to contact local real estate brokers in the area who may have a better sense of what properties are about to come to market. Real estate agents can be an important partner in finding a property.

Your property selection will largely depend on the numbers. Especially if you're looking for an investment property versus a property that you're going to live in, you're not going to buy based on the paint color or what kind of landscaping surrounds the yard. While these aesthetics can play a role in determining the rent you might be able to fetch for the place, your decision to buy a certain property depends on the profitability. Worry about the numbers versus the ugly bright green walls in one of the bedrooms.

How do you run the numbers? Well, first here's a brief rundown of the costs that are typically involved in buying a rental investment property:

- **Mortgage:** This is pretty straightforward. There are many mortgage calculators online that will tell you your monthly payment based on the home's purchase price and the interest rate you plan to pay on your mortgage. Mortgage interest rates are also widely available online.
- **Insurance:** You are going to need homeowner's insurance, just like you would with any home you purchase. However, as a landlord, you want to have some sort of liability insurance. Simply call insurance companies in your area and explain your situation—how you plan to buy a home and rent it out. Landlord liability insurance is important because if someone trips and falls on your property and they end

up suing you (maybe the front steps were damaged and created a dangerous situation), your insurance company may be able to settle with the plaintiff. Insurance can give you peace of mind. Or maybe you didn't have a proper railing on the steps leading into the basement and a tenant falls and breaks his leg and now cannot go to work for the next several years. He may sue you for damages. This can be a financially devastating event for you if you do not have liability insurance.

- **Water bill:** Sometimes, you, as the owner are required to pay the water bill. This may depend on the city where the property is located. But it's a cost to consider. The last thing you want is to be stuck with an unexpected expense *after* you purchase the property. Know before you buy: Who pays the water bill? You or the tenants? Do some research; ask local real estate agents how it works. You can even call the local water company to find out more information. They may even be able to tell you what the water has been in previous years at a specific address. This way you don't have to estimate the water bill cost when you run the numbers on your property to see how much it cash flows each month. The more accurate you are with estimating the expenses, the more accurate the estimate you'll have on the monthly cash flow, which is the most important number in this entire equation.

- **Utilities:** It's pretty common for the tenants to pay the electric bill, but if most of the other rental properties in the neighborhood are offering free utilities to the tenants (i.e., the owner pays them), you may have to offer the same to stay competitive. In that case, you would need to update your cash flow spreadsheet (more on this in a moment) to account for this extra expense. Again, the utility company in your area may be able to share with you the average utility bill for a specific property. This allows you to use a more accurate estimate when you run the numbers for the property.

- **Property taxes:** As an owner, you're going to have to pay property taxes. These are public record, so you can easily look up the property taxes for a given address.

- **Vacancy:** It's a common rule of thumb to set aside 10 percent of a property's monthly rental revenue for the possibility of the house or apartment being vacant. Vacant means no tenants are living in the property, and, more important, vacant means no revenue is coming into your bank account each month. What if you can't rent the place right away? Or your tenant stops paying rent for a few months? If your rent is $1,000 a month, set aside $100 per month for this possibility—that's 10 percent. Think of it as another line item on your expense list, like taxes or the water bill. Even if you are buying a property that is already rented with existing tenants, eventually one of them is going to move out and you may find yourself with a few months of vacancy. Think of this vacancy line item as a rainy day fund for your investment property.

- **Repairs:** This is difficult to estimate and it will largely depend on the age of the house and how well your tenants take care of the property. It is difficult to advise on what portion of the monthly rent should be set aside in reserves each month because there are so many variables. But it is better to be conservative, that is, set aside more money than less money for these unknown repairs. This will make your cash flow numbers look worse on paper, but that's okay. You never know when the toilet will break, when the washing machine needs repairs, or when the tenant accidentally leaves the water running in the upstairs bathroom sink and floods the entire downstairs. Anything is possible! Remember, your tenant doesn't own the property. Hopefully, they are honorable and will treat the property as if they did own it. But you could have a careless tenant who damages the place.

- **CAPEX:** This stands for capital expenditures. This is different from repairs in that we're not talking about a $50 plumbing bill but potentially a $50,000 roof. A roof can last a few decades. Assuming you own the property over the long term, chances are you'll need to eventually pay for a new roof. Your home inspector should be able to give you a sense of the roof's current age. If you are buying a house with a roof that is in working order but is very old and needs to be replaced soon, you may want to try to negotiate money off of the purchase price to put toward the eventual repair. If the house's roof doesn't need to be replaced for another 10 years, the expense isn't imminent. But in the CAPEX section of your cash flow statement, you would set aside money each month to be put toward the long-term CAPEX of the property, including a new roof, a new furnace, a new hot water heater, new appliances, and new windows, among other big ticket items. So take the roof, for example. If a new roof costs $30,000 and you're not going to need a new roof for another 10 years, that's $3,000 per year that you should be setting aside for the eventual roof replacement (30,000/10 = 3,000). Per month, that's $250 that should be set aside in your CAPEX reserve. And that's just the roof. You are likely going to have other big-ticket repairs—again, such as a new hot water heater, a new furnace, etc. The CAPEX section of your cash flow statement will make your numbers look worse, but then again, your rental income is supposed to cover these costs. Budgeting for these long-term items just helps you avoid getting blindsided with a big CAPEX bill over the next few years. The reality is that you're eventually going to have these big repair costs, so you might as well start budgeting for them now.

- **Management:** This cost is entirely up to you. If you want to be the one managing the property, you just need to be prepared to put in the hours. Your tenants may call

you with repair requests, noise complaints,
complaints about the neighbors—you name
it! You may need to coordinate other services,
like hiring snow removal personnel (or
shoveling the snow yourself!) or coordinating
the use of exterminators in case tenants call
with complaints of bugs. Rent collection
is also another key component of property
management. There are plenty of books on how
to be an efficient property manager, but if you
are going to hire a property manager, expect
them to take 7 to 10 percent of the monthly
rent as a fee, sometimes even more. Also, select
your property manager very carefully, because
you're probably going to be putting a lot of
trust in their ability to manage the property
efficiently and handle any issues that come
up. Ask for references! Interview more than
one prospective property manager. Also, if the
property is located far away from you, that
may make your decision to hire a property
manager even more obvious because managing
a property yourself from afar is difficult.

You may try to manage the property on your own, especially if it's near where you live. But if your real estate endeavors become successful and you start to accumulate multiple properties, it's probably not realistic for you to manage several properties on your own. That's why even if you manage the first property on your own to save the 7 to 10 percent management fee, you may want to run the numbers as if you had hired the manager in case you decide to hire a property manager later on.

So the financial characteristics of the investment should work even with the 7 to 10 percent management fee. Obviously, the numbers are going to be better without this expense, but it's important that the property is still profitable once you add on the extra cost of property management. Basically, if the only way the property cash flows (gives you profit each month!) is if you manage the property on your own, thereby saving you the 7 to 10 percent management fee, it may be worth continuing your search for another investment property. Maybe the one you're looking at has too high of a purchase price.

Will Your Property Be Profitable?

Using an online spreadsheet program, here is how you can clearly outline your property's revenue (the money coming in each month) and its expenses (the money you have to pay to own and maintain the property) *before* you buy it:

Property Address:
123 Example Avenue

Financials:

Purchase price	$90,000
Down payment (25%)	$22,500

Monthly Revenue:

Rent	$1,600

Monthy Expenses:

Mortgage payment	$400
Property taxes	$200
Vacancy	$150
CAPEX	$150

Management Fee	$150
Water bill	$50
Utilities	$0
Maintenance	$200
Total Expenses:	$1,300

**Cash Flow (monthy revenue
minus total expenses):** $300

This is a simple and easy way to organize your property's financial characteristics. All of this information is available as you are looking at prospective properties. You wouldn't buy a property and then run the numbers to see if it works! If a property that you're looking at is already rented, you can ask the owner or the real estate agent for a copy of the current leases or the rent roll, which is a document that states how much each unit rents for. A property that is already rented means you'll have revenue as soon as you take ownership of the property, which is a positive. But the downside is, you did not choose the tenants and it's really hard to know if the existing tenants pay the rent on time and take reasonable steps to maintain the health of the property. If the property is not rented, ask the real estate agent for their best estimate on what the unit might rent for. You can also look online at what other rentals in the neighborhood are getting in terms of price that are of similar size and quality to your prospective rental.

The property taxes are public record. The maintenance, CAPEX, and vacancy costs are forecasts. It's hard to know what maintenance costs you'll experience during your time as the new owner of the property, and it's difficult to gauge how long it will take to find tenants to rent the property.

A Key Characteristic of Cash Flow

For purposes of this discussion, cash flow is the money left over after paying all your expenses. Now, as stated earlier, some of the expenses in the example above aren't necessarily "out-of-pocket" expenses. With the vacancy, you're not writing a check to someone for $150 a month, you're just pretending to because you want to be conservative and assume that the property won't be fully occupied year-round.

It's the same concept with CAPEX and maintenance—you may have to use all of this money or half of this money or none of this money. It depends on what maintenance costs come up, and there's just no way to know this. In this example, your cash flow is higher than $300 per month. But at some point, these "imaginary" expenses may pop up. For now, let's just stick with the forecast of a $300 monthly cash flow on this investment.

When it comes to trying to quickly figure out if a property will cash flow or not, try this rule of thumb: if the monthly rental revenue of the property is less than 1 percent of the purchase price, the property is probably not going to cash flow. It may cash flow negative! Meaning the costs of the property are more than the revenue. Ideally, you want the monthly rental revenue to be between 1-2 percent of the purchase price.

This is why the process of finding the right property to invest in is arguably the hardest part of real estate investing. Even if the rent is 1 percent of the purchase price, it still may not cash flow enough for you to be excited about investing in the property.

In the example above, the rent is $1,600 per month and the purchase price is $90,000. If we divide 1,600 by

90,000, the result is 0.0177. Multiply this figure by 100 and you get 1.77 percent, which is right in the sweet spot of the 1 to 2 percent rule of thumb. Because of this ratio, it's no surprise that the property cash flows by several hundred dollars per month.

But if your monthly rent divided by the purchase price gives you a number of less than 1 percent, once you run the entire spreadsheet of numbers, you'll probably find that you are cash flow negative or break even. This is a quick way to figure out if a property cash flows before you start pulling all of the different numbers in the chart.

This rule can be a helpful way to screen different properties. If they meet the rule, then you can run the entire spreadsheet above and actually figure out the exact cash flow. But if the property doesn't meet the rule, it may not make sense to go through the entire spreadsheet process only to find out that your property loses $100 per month.

As I write this in 2019, real estate prices in many cities across the country have surged over the past eight years or so. While rents have risen too, in many cities, the rents just aren't high enough to justify such a high purchase price. Meaning, if the purchase price is high, your mortgage payment will be high, and the rental revenue just may not be high enough to cover all of the property's monthly expenses.

As an investor, you need to find a property that doesn't cost too much, but that's also in a good neighborhood where the properties command strong rents. It's challenging to find this.

If you can't find any properties that seem appealing from a financial point of view, don't get discouraged! You can keep looking. There is no need to jump into a property that's not a great investment just for the sake of becoming a real estate investor. There are plenty of real estate blogs, books, and podcasts out there that glorify real estate investing. I'm not saying it can't be a good investment, but there are pitfalls. Some of the real estate investing advice content I've come across on the internet seems to downplay the pitfalls and only focus on the good things. Some of the content almost makes you feel stupid if you're not a real estate investor! You don't need to subscribe to the hype.

Worst-case scenario—you wait to buy a property and save up more money in the meantime. There's nothing wrong with building up your cash stockpile.

Lease Agreements

I'm sure you've heard the common advice of "get it in writing." The same principle can apply to the relationship between a landlord (you, the owner) and a tenant. Even if your tenant is on a month-to-month tenancy— meaning they can vacate the property at any time without any penalties (usually a tenant has to give a landlord 30 days' notice), having the terms of the relationship in writing can save you a lot of hassle should the relationship sour. Talk to a lawyer about drafting a lease agreement for your tenant.

As a landlord, you want certainty. While there's no way to guarantee that your tenant will pay the rent, having a one-year lease is better than a month-to-month lease. With a one-year lease, the tenant typically cannot simply vacate the property without at least paying the remaining months rent under the term. So if the tenant tries to terminate the lease four months into a one-year term, generally, they must pay you eight months' worth of rent. This is a disincentive for them to break the lease. Now just because the lease states that they cannot break the lease early, doesn't mean they won't. If that happens, you would have to make a business and legal decision—do you sue the tenant? Is it worth the legal costs and hassle? It might be. You could argue that the terms of a contract are meaningless—unless you sue and a judge rules in your favor. That doesn't mean you do away with a contract. Because should you find yourself in a situation where you are suing a tenant or a tenant is suing you, chances are, the contract will come in handy.

Security Deposit

This is another important legal issue: a tenant's security deposit. Landlords hold a certain amount of money from a tenant to be used to pay for any potential damages to the property throughout a tenant's time living there. The security deposit is largely a deterrent for a tenant to damage the property. If a tenant decides to move a dresser to the other side of the room and scratches the floor as a result, you, the landlord, may be able to keep a portion of the security deposit to fix the floor. Knowing this, a tenant may think twice before moving the dresser—or at least take some measures to ensure the floors don't get damaged in that process.

A tenant's security deposit is not yours to keep. A landlord must return it to the tenant once they move out. If there are damages, you can communicate that to the tenant and explain why you are keeping $250 of the $1,000 security deposit to pay a professional to fix the damages they caused to the floor.

Making an Offer—Getting a Good Deal Is Key

When investing in real estate, the purchase price is incredibly important. Just because your property is going to produce income for you each month doesn't mean you shouldn't try to get the best price on the home. Negotiation is still a critical part of investing in real estate. A lower purchase price will also translate into higher monthly cash flow and a thicker profit margin should you decide to sell your investment property in a few years. While monthly cash flow is important, so is some price appreciation on the actual property. You give yourself a stronger chance of price appreciation when you get a better deal on the initial purchase price of the property.

Finding the Right Neighborhood

A great starting place for investment properties can be the neighborhood you live in. Now if you live in a high-cost city like New York City or San Francisco, this may be tough. Prices can be so high in these cities (the rents aren't cheap either) that it may be very difficult to meet the 1 to 2 percent cash flow rule we talked about earlier. If you happen to live in a city with a lower cost of living, perhaps you will have better luck finding investment opportunities.

Generally speaking, you want to see a few characteristics in a neighborhood: low unemployment and population growth. How are your tenants going to pay the rent if they aren't employed? You can usually check a city's unemployment rate online. You also want to know which companies are the major employers in the area. If, for example, one auto company provides most of the jobs in a city, well, if that auto company shuts down the plant or facility in that city, you could see sky-high unemployment within days. A diversified local economy is best (that is, there are multiple large employers in the area).

Conducting a quick internet search for local news articles that discuss which companies are moving into or exiting in the area can be helpful. If you notice that some major tech companies are setting up shop in a particular city, well, that is a sign of upside ahead.

Population growth is also important and is tied to employment. If a city has rising population growth over time, that suggests there will likely be more demand for housing. You have to live somewhere, right? If people are moving into a city in droves, that may push up the price of rentals, which means more cash flow for you.

Try to examine the historical characteristics of a city's economy. Soon after the financial crisis of 2008, the economy started to recover in a dramatic way. But maybe some cities had a delayed economic recovery. Maybe a city's particular economy didn't start to recover until 2011 or 2012. Even if a particular city's unemployment rate is higher than the average of the state or even the national average, that doesn't mean buying a property there is a bad investment. If the trend of the unemployment rate is down, that's a good sign. After all, you don't necessarily want to buy a property during the boom time—that's when prices tend to be highest. It may be better to acquire the asset when a city is first starting to recover from an economic headwind and ride the trend higher with it. Now, obviously, this kind of "market timing" is very hard to do.

As of October 2019, CoreLogic's Home Price Index has increased 62.5 percent since its March 2011 bottom.[3] That gives you an idea of just how much home prices have surged in the United States over the past several years. Now if you had purchased a home in 2011, you likely scored a pretty hefty property value gain, at least on paper.

But how does the United States real estate property surge over the past decade or so compare to how stocks have performed over the same time? Well, in March 2011, the Dow Jones Industrial Average was at roughly 12,100 give or take.[4] Fast-forward to January 2020 and it was trading near 29,000.[5] That's an increase of about 140 percent. That's double that of the aforementioned real estate gain during the same time.

Short-Term Rentals

Another corner of the real estate market is short-term rentals. This is essentially where you purchase an investment property and instead of renting it to a long-term tenant on a one-year lease, you would list the home on a short-term rental listing website (you probably have been on these sites before or at least heard of them). Here, you would charge a *nightly* rate for the property, like a hotel does. Depending on the property, you may be able to make more money via short-term rentals than long-term tenants.

There is, however, a lot of uncertainty with this strategy. That's because it is very hard to know how vacant your property will be. Even though you may be able to score some hefty nightly rates for your property, if the property is only rented two weeks out of the month, well, you might not be making more than if the property was just rented to a long-term tenant at a lower rate—at least it would be filled with a tenant for that year and the vacancy would be zero.

Here are the risks with short-term rentals:

1. **Vacancy:** Short-term rentals are unpredictable. Some months you might have guests every night and other months you may have guests only half the month.

2. **Pricing:** Just like a hotel, the pricing can change nightly based on supply and demand. If there's a major convention one weekend in your city, you will likely be able to charge a higher rate for your property due to higher demand. But that may just be an infrequent sugar high to the pricing. Plus, short-term rentals can be seasonal, depending on the location. For example, take a short-term rental in Florida. The pricing tends to drop in the summer months when it's very hot outside but then surges in the winter months, as people flock to Florida from the North to escape the cold weather. You may be making money in the winter, but in the summer months, when prices drop, you may only be breaking even on your property.

3. **Damage to property:** Even if your guests cause no problems (and that's a big if!), think of the normal wear and tear the property may suffer with a new guest coming in every week. Renting your property out on short-term rental sites

may require you to set aside more money for routine maintenance.

4. **Regulation:** Some cities allow short-term rentals with open arms. Others have significant restrictions on short-term rentals. That's because some neighborhoods may not want to have a "hotel" property nestled between a bunch of single-family homes. Some cities only allow you to list your home on a short-term rental website for a maximum of 30 to 60 nights per year. This can be great if you're taking a two-week trip to Europe and you want your property to produce some income while you're gone. However, you can't create an actual short-term rental business if you are only allowed to rent the property for 30 to 60 days per year.

   Regulation is a significant risk for investors relying on short-term rentals. Just because a city allows it now, that doesn't mean they will allow it in six months or one year from now. Rules change. If you are very passionate about the short term rental strategy, try running the numbers on your property to see if it will still cash flow from a long-term tenant. Before investing, it's important to understand if the property will work in both capacities: short term and long term. If your city changes the rules, at least you can pivot to a long-term rental and still receive some monthly cash flow, even if it's less than what you would have received in a short-term rental capacity.

5. **Furnishings:** With a long-term rental, usually the tenant brings their own furniture. With a

short-term rental, you have to provide not just furniture and, likely, a television, but also towels, kitchen utensils, and pretty much anything one would reasonably expect to have when staying in someone's home. Your short-term rental is competing with dozens of others in your neighborhood. If you don't have a television with cable and Wi-Fi, you may lose out to the competition. There are obviously costs associated with furnishing an entire house. Plus, if your property doesn't have the amenities that guests expect, you run the risk of the guest writing a bad review of your property on the short-term rental website. The short-term listing websites have a review section, where guests can share details about their experience. If your listing has poor ratings and reviews, it may deter future guests from booking your property.

6. **Utilities:** With short-term rentals, usually a guest will stay for one night or three nights or 10 nights. They could blast your air conditioning and keep all the lights on all day. That would increase your electric bill. In a long-term rental, however, it is common for the tenant to pay the utilities. So if they fail to turn off the lights and air conditioning when not in use, those costs will come out of their pocket and not yours.

7. **Fees:** Typically, the short-term rental website takes a percentage of your nightly fee, sometimes a few percentage points. This is the cost of doing business. But it's just something to be aware of.

8. **Management:** Managing a short-term rental is arguably a job in itself. You could have a new

guest coming every week! You need to some-
how give them the key to the property—there
are electronic keys you can install to make it easier. But you still have to coordinate some sort of
cleaning service to clean the property between
guests, and you may need to be on call should
the guest have any issues. You can hire a manager to oversee this entire property, but don't
be surprised if a property manager charges a
much higher fee to manage a short-term rental
rather than a long-term rental. Why? Because
short-term rentals tend to be more work. This
extra fee eats into your profits.

It's hard to say what the better option is: short-term
or long-term rental. There are pros and cons to each.
Keep in mind, the information so far about short-term
rentals largely applies to the idea of purchasing a property with the goal of renting it on a short-term rental
website for as many nights as you can. If you wanted to
rent out a room in your existing home—that is completely different. That is not an investment so to speak
but it can be a great way to bring in some extra money
each month.

Low Volatility in Real Estate Investing

With real estate investing, you get a rent check each
month from your tenants. You pay your property's
monthly expenses (mortgage, maintenance, property
taxes, the property management fee) and what is leftover
is your cash flow—that's yours to keep. The only way this

process would stop is if your tenant moved out and you failed to find a new tenant—or if your existing tenant just stopped paying rent. In that case, you would likely start a legal process to remove them from the property (i.e., eviction).

Still, there is something to say about that stable monthly rental check. Especially if you have your tenants on a one-year lease, you know that you won't really have to worry about finding a new tenant until that lease expires.

With the stock market you may be able to score a higher return, but there can be a lot of volatility with stocks, which means lots of changes in prices. One day your stocks can be up big and the next day you could be down big. Over time, the average return in the stock market is respectable, but if you are the type who likes to check your investments on a daily basis, seeing that day-to-day volatility can be frightening. So if you can't handle the volatility of the stock market, it may make sense to diversify some of your investments to real estate.

Then again, even with real estate, if you had to sell your property, it can take months or even years to do so. With stocks, you can sell your holdings in a matter of seconds.

Another Note on Relativity in Investing

Real estate can be one part of your overall portfolio. Real estate is simply another tool in your investing toolbox to build wealth and achieve the financial independence needed to survive in the event of a world with sky-high unemployment due to the rise of artificial intelligence. Investing doesn't have to be all or nothing. You don't have to put all of your money in real estate, and you don't have to put all of your money in stocks.

You run the show.

Quick Review

This was a pretty comprehensive compilation of the main ways that investing in real estate can provide the steady, monthly cash flow you need to achieve financial independence. Here are some of the main takeaways from this chapter:

1. When it comes to the home you live in, don't feel ashamed about renting. In some cities, it may make more sense to rent versus buy and instead focus on investing in the stock market.
2. Real estate investing can be a great way to diversify your income streams away from your 9-to-5 daily job and stock dividends. Learning how to "run the numbers" is a key part of any real estate investment deal to make sure the property is paying you each month versus the other way around.
3. Real estate investing comes with risk: What if the tenant doesn't pay the rent? What if your property doesn't appreciate in price as much as you expected?
4. Don't rush into buying a property: the price must be right!

Billionaires and Financial Independence

Billionaires. They are mega-rich people. They can buy a private jet; they can buy the biggest house; they can buy almost anything they want. There are actually 2,101 billionaires across the globe, according to a 2019 UBS report.[1] Think about how many billions of people are on this planet and only a few thousand have billionaire status. The notion of income inequality and billionaires having too much and not paying enough in taxes has been a big issue in the 2020 US presidential race. It has become a popular talking point among some presidential candidates to suggest plans on taxing some of the richest Americans. This book is not about that or the politics behind the billionaire class.

Intersection of Billionaires and Financial Independence

So what do billionaires have to do with your financial independence? Well, not much. But I think you would be surprised to hear about how some billionaires advocate frugality!

In an interview with *Money* published in 2017, billionaire Mark Cuban talked about the need to have discipline when dealing with finances and talked about his frugality in the early years of his career:[2] "I did things like having five roommates and living off of macaroni and cheese, and I was very, very frugal," he said. "I had the worst possible car—those types of things."

Mark Cuban, owner of the Dallas Mavericks, is a well-known business person and has an estimated net worth of $4.1 billion, according to *Forbes*,[3] as of January 2020.

Cuban went on to discuss his passion for saving money:[4] "I was determined to save money. I was determined to be able to retire," he said. "It wasn't like I thought, 'Okay, I'm going to be super-rich.'"

He, of course, ended up becoming super-rich.

In the same interview with *Money*, billionaire entrepreneur Sara Blakely, founder of Spanx, also discussed her frugal ways, saying:[5] "My main thing is I just spend below my means. And as my means change, maybe what I can spend changes, but I always keep that as my baseline. If I'm spending well below my means, I'm going to be in good shape." According to Forbes,[6] Blakely's estimated net worth is $1.1 billion.

It is remarkable to hear stories like these of very successful people talking about the importance of saving money. The key takeaway here is that saving money and financial independence in and of itself is not that difficult. It does, however, require a tremendous will power and determination to take the necessary steps to cut your spending, invest wisely, and build up a nest egg of assets. Oh, and patience. Building a mountain of assets is by no means an overnight process.

You Don't Need to Become a Billionaire

Will eating mac and cheese and always living below your means turn you into a billionaire? Probably not. The aforementioned billionaires started businesses—that's how they accumulated their wealth. But the good news is, you don't have to achieve billionaire status in order to be financially independent or financially successful. Don't be discouraged; this information aims to give you some perspective—that some of the world's most successful and richest people are talking about the importance of saving money.

Even Warren Buffett knows this. When he was about 25 years old, he had $127,000—this was at the end of 1955—according to an article he wrote for *Forbes* in 2012.[7] Remember, as of January 2020, Warren Buffett's estimated net worth was $89.4 billion, according to *Forbes*.[8] That's quite a difference! But Buffett wrote that at 25 he was considering retiring:[9] "I was going to retire! I figured we could live on $12,000 a year, and off my $127,000 asset base, I could easily make that. I told my wife, 'Compound interest guarantees I'm going to get rich.'"

Isn't that remarkable: compound interest guarantees wealth! And this was long before Buffett became one of the world's richest persons. It's fascinating to see a business and financial titan like Warren Buffett talk about his awareness of the benefits of compound interest decades before he became a billionaire.

Quick Review

The goal of this chapter was to show you that even rich people—or people who became very rich—think about frugality and saving money. Again, scrimping and saving won't exactly make you a billionaire, but over time it could make you a millionaire. That wouldn't be so bad, right? Here are a few takeaways from this chapter:

1. Rich people think about frugality too.
2. Take saving money seriously!

Conclusion

And that's a wrap. Thank you for reading. If you take anything away from the book, it's that saving money and investing are two key ingredients for financial independence. Even if you don't have a lot of money to save or invest, starting small is likely to pay nice dividends over the long term.

As for the artificial intelligence angle, it doesn't make any sense to worry about it in the short term. What does make sense is to constantly take steps to ensure that your finances are in working order so that you're prepared for whatever life may throw at you: whether it's a job loss due to artificial intelligence, a routine corporate layoff, or an illness that prevents you from working.

Achieving financial independence status doesn't mean you have to stop working. You may want to continue working to attain an even thicker financial cushion, or you may want to take a leap and pursue something you're passionate about or finally start the business of your dreams.

Endnotes

Chapter 1: Financial Independence and Artificial Intelligence

1. Richard Branson, "The Way We All Work Is Going to Change," *Virgin,* December 12, 2018, https://www.virgin.com/richard-branson/way-we-all-work-going-change.
2. "Machines Will Do More Tasks Than Humans by 2025, but Robot Revolution Will Still Create 58 Million Net New Jobs in Next Five Years," World Economic Forum, September 17, 2018, http://reports.weforum.org/future-of-jobs-2018/press-releases/.
3. Ibid.
4. "IBM Study: The Skills Gap Is Not a Myth, but Can Be Addressed with Real Solutions," IBM Newsroom, September 6, 2019, https://newsroom.ibm.com/2019-09-06-IBM-Study-The-Skills-Gap-is-Not-a-Myth-But-Can-Be-Addressed-with-Real-Solutions.
5. "Amazon Pledges to Upskill 100,000 U.S. Employees for In-Demand Jobs by 2025," Amazon Press Center, July 11, 2019, https://press.aboutamazon.com/news-releases/news-release-details/amazon-pledges-upskill-100000-us-employees-demand-jobs-2025.

6. "Preparing Everyone, Everywhere, for the Digital World," PricewaterhouseCoopers, accessed October 5, 2019, https://www.pwc.com/gx/en/issues/ups killing/everyone-digital-world.html.
7. "JPMorgan Chase Makes $350 Million Global Investment in the Future of Work," JPMorgan Chase & Co, March 18, 2019, https://www.jpmorganchase.com/corporate/news/pr/jpmorgan-chase-global-investment-in-the-future-of-work.htm.
8. "Department of Technology," Yang 2020, accessed November 30, 2020, https://www.yang2020.com/policies/regulating-ai-emerging-technologies/.
9. Ibid.
10. Laura Noonan, "Deutsche Boss Cryan Warns of 'Big Number' of Job Losses from Tech Change," *Financial Times,* September 6, 2017, https://www.ft.com/content/62ee1265-dce7-352f-b103-6eeb74 7d4998.

Chapter 2: What Does Artificial Intelligence Mean for the Gig Economy?

1. "Uber Technologies, Inc. (UBER)," Yahoo Finance, accessed January 12, 2020, https://finance.yahoo.com/quote/UBER?p=UBER&.tsrc=fin-srch.
2. "Lyft, Inc. (LYFT)," Yahoo Finance, accessed January 12, 2020, https://finance.yahoo.com/quote/LYFT?p=LYFT&.tsrc=fin-srch.
3. "Advanced Technologies Group," Uber, accessed January 12, 2020, https://www.uber.com/us/en/atg/.
4. Arun Sundararajan (professor at New York University's Stern School of Business and author of *The*

Sharing Economy: The End of Employment and the Rise of Crowd-Based Capitalism), interview by author, January 6, 2020.
5. Ibid.

Chapter 3: The Robots Determine How Much Money You Need to Retire

1. "Employment Situation Summary," Bureau of Labor Statistics, October 4, 2019, https://www.bls.gov /news.release/empsit.nr0.htm.
2. "Personal Income and Outlays, August 2019," Bureau of Economic Analysis, September, 27, 2019, https:// www.bea.gov/news/2019/personal-income-and -outlays-august-2019.
3. "Personal Income and Outlays, August 2009," Bureau of Economic Analysis, October 1, 2009, https:// www.bea.gov/news/2009/personal-income-and -outlays-august-2009.
4. "FIRE Movement Enthusiasts Say FI (Financial Independence) Outranks RE (Retire Early)," BusinessWire, December 13, 2018, https://www.business wire.com/news/home/20181213005026/en/.
5. Cooper J. Howard and Rob Williams, "Beyond the 4% Rule: How Much Can You Spend in Retirement?" Charles Schwab, March 12, 2019, https:// www.schwab.com/resource-center/insights /content/beyond-4-rule-how-much-can-you -safely-spend-retirement.
6. Ibid.
7. "Consumer Price Index Summary," Bureau of Labor Statistics, October 10, 2019, https://www.bls.gov /news.release/cpi.nr0.htm.

8. "National Health Expenditures 2018 Highlights," Historical, Centers for Medicare & Medicaid Services, December 17, 2019, https://www.cms.gov /Research-Statistics-Data-and-Systems/Statistics -Trends-and-Reports/NationalHealthExpendData /NationalHealthAccountsHistorical.html.

Chapter 4: How to Prepare for the "Artificial Intelligence Tax"

1. "Affordable Housing," Community Planning and Development, Department of Housing and Urban Development, accessed October 15, 2019, hud .gov/program_offices/comm_planning/affordable housing/.
2. "What Is a Good Credit Score?" Experian, October 16, 2019, https://www.experian.com/blogs/ask -experian/credit-education/score-basics/what-is-a -good-credit-score/.

Chapter 5: Debt and Robots Don't Mix

1. "The Consumer Credit Card Market," Bureau of Consumer Financial Protection, August 2019, https://files.consumerfinance.gov/f/documents /cfpb_consumer-credit-card-market-report_2019 .pdf.
2. "Credit Card Lending," Office of the Comptroller of the Currency, November 2015, https://www.occ .treas.gov/publications-and-resources/publications /comptrollers-handbook/files/credit-card-lending /index-credit-card-lending.html; 34.

3. "Credit Card Minimum Payment Calculator: How Long Will It Take to Pay Off Credit Cards?," Bankrate, October 20, 2019, https://www.bankrate.com/calculators/credit-cards/credit-card-minimum-payment.aspx.

4. "Quarterly Report on Household Debt and Credit," Federal Reserve Bank of New York, Research and Statistics Group, August 2019, https://www.newyorkfed.org/medialibrary/interactives/householdcredit/data/pdf/hhdc_2019q2.pdf.

5. "Report on the Economic Well-Being of U.S. Households in 2018," Student Loans and Other Education Debt, Board of Governors of the Federal Reserve System, last modified May 28, 2019, (accessed October 21, 2019), https://www.federalreserve.gov/publications/2019-economic-well-being-of-us-households-in-2018-student-loans-and-other-education-debt.htm.

6. "PLUS Loans for Parents," Federal Student Aid, accessed October 21, 2019, https://studentaid.ed.gov/sa/types/loans/plus/parent#how-much.

7. "Standard Plan," Federal Student Aid, accessed October 21, 2019, https://studentaid.ed.gov/sa/repay-loans/understand/plans/standard#eligible-loans.

8. "Extended Plan," Federal Student Aid, accessed October 21, 2019, https://studentaid.ed.gov/sa/repay-loans/understand/plans≈xtended.

9. "PLUS Loans for Parents," Federal Student Aid, accessed October 21, 2019, https://studentaid.ed.gov/sa/types/loans/plus/parent#eligibility.

10. Katie Lobosco, "New Employee Perk: $100 a Month for Your Student Loans," CNN Money, October

19, 2017, https://money.cnn.com/2017/10/19/pf /college/student-loan-benefit-pwc/index.html.

11. "Quarterly Report on Household Debt and Credit," Federal Reserve Bank of NewYork, Research and Statistics Group, August 2019, https://www.newyorkfed .org/medialibrary/interactives/householdcredit/data/pdf /hhdc_2019q2.pdf.

12. "Mortgage Rates Jump," Mortgage Rates, Freddie Mac, October 17, 2019, http://www.freddiemac.com /pmms/.

Chapter 6: Understanding the Stock Market

1. Investopedia, "Affluent Millennials Don't Think They'll Retire by 65," PR Newswire, October 2, 2019, https://www.prnewswire.com/news-releases /affluent-millennials-dont-think-theyll-retire-by -65-300929551.html.

2. "The Home Depot, Inc." (HD), Yahoo Finance, accessed January 18, 2020, https://finance.yahoo.com /quote/HD?p=HD&.tsrc=fin-srch.

3. Ibid.

4. "2018 Annual Report," Berkshire Hathaway, Inc., February 23, 2019, https://www.berkshirehathaway .com/2018ar/2018ar.pdf.

5. "Investors Info: Dividends," Coca Cola, October 23, 2019, https://www.coca-colacompany.com/investors /investors-info-dividends.

6. "SPDR® S&P 500® ETF Trust," State Street Global Advisors, November 24, 2019, https://us.spdrs.com /en/etf/spdr-sp-500-etf-trust-SPY.

7. "2018 Annual Report," Berkshire Hathaway, Inc.

8. Ibid.

9. "S&P 500," S&P Dow Jones Indices, accessed October 29, 2019, https://us.spindices.com/indices /equity/sp-500.
10. Alexandra Twin, "For Dow, Another 12-Year Low," CNN Money, March 9, 2009, https://money.cnn .com/2009/03/09/markets/markets_newyork/.
11. "S&P 500 (^GSPC)," Yahoo Finance, accessed January 18, 2020, https://finance.yahoo.com/quote/% 5EGSPC?p=^GSPC&.tsrc=fin-srch.
12. "Dow Jones Industrial Average," S&P Dow Jones Indices, accessed October 29, 2019, https://us .spindices.com/indices/equity/dow-jones-industrial -average.
13. "2016 Annual Report," Berkshire Hathaway, Inc., February 25, 2017, http://www.berkshirehathaway .com/letters/2016ltr.pdf.
14. "#3: Warren Buffett," *Forbes,* October 30, 2019, https://www.forbes.com/profile/warren-buffett/# 74c536b46398.
15. "2016 Annual Report," Berkshire Hathaway, Inc.
16. "Employment Situation Summary," Economic News Release, Bureau of Labor Statistics, January 10, 2020.
17. "Gross Domestic Product," Bureau of Economic Analysis, last modified January 18, 2020, https:// www.bea.gov/resources/learning-center/what-to -know-gdp.
18. "Recession," Bureau of Economic Analysis, last modified January 18, 2020, https://www.bea.gov /help/glossary/recession.
19. "Advance Monthly Sales for Retail and Food Services, December 2019," Census.gov, January 16, 2020, https://www.census.gov/retail/marts/www/marts _current.pdf.

20. "About the Fed," Board of Governors of the Federal Reserve System, accessed January 18, 2020, https://www.federalreserve.gov/aboutthefed.htm.
21. "Federal Funds Data," Federal Reserve Bank of New York, accessed March 14, 2020, https://apps.newyorkfed.org/markets/autorates/fed%20funds.
22. Patrick Gillespie. "Finally! Fed Raises Interest Rates," CNN Business, December 16, 2015, https://money.cnn.com/2015/12/16/news/economy/federal-reserve-interest-rate-hike/.

Chapter 7: What Artificial Intelligence May Mean for 401(k)s

1. "401(k) Plan Overview," Internal Revenue Service, last modified December 4, 2019 (last updated).
2. "How AI and Robotics May Change Tax Job Duties," Ernst & Young Global, July 2, 2019, https://www.ey.com/en_gl/tax/how-ai-and-robotics-may-change-tax-job-duties.
3. "401(k) Contribution Limit Increases to $19,500 for 2020; Catch-Up Limit Rises to $6,500," Internal Revenue Service, November, 6, 2019, https://www.irs.gov/newsroom/401k-contribution-limit-increases-to-19500-for-2020-catch-up-limit-rises-to-6500.
4. "Bill Gates Thinks We Should Tax the Robot That Takes Your Job," interview by Quartz, February 16, 2017, https://www.youtube.com/watch?v=nccryZOcrUg.
5. "De Blasio Campaign Launches 'Robot Tax' as Part of Aggressive Plan to Protect Workers from Threat of Automation," de Blasio 2020, September

5, 2019, https://billdeblasio.com/press/in-the-news
-automation-plan/.
6. "2014 Annual Report," Berkshire Hathaway, Inc.,
February 27, 2015, https://www.berkshirehathaway
.com/letters/2014ltr.pdf.
7. "Roth IRAs," Internal Revenue Service, last modified January 10, 2020, https://www.irs.gov/retirement
-plans/roth-iras.

Chapter 8: Real Estate and Financial Independence

1. Robert J. Shiller (Sterling Professor of Economics at
Yale University, a 2013 Nobel laureate in economics, and author of *Narrative Economics: How Stories
Go Viral and Drive Major Economic Events*), interview
by author, November 6, 2019.
2. Ibid.
3. Molly Boesel. "U.S. Prices Level Off, Some States
Show Large Cooldown," CoreLogic Insights (blog),
December 3, 2019, https://www.corelogic.com/blog
/2019/11/us-prices-level-off-some-states-show
-large-cooldown.aspx.
4. "Dow Jones Industrial Average (^DJI)," Yahoo
Finance, accessed January 25, 2020.
5. Ibid.

Chapter 9: Billionaires and Financial Independence

1. "The Billionaire Effect," UBS Group AG, last
modified November 2019, https://www.ubs.com
/global/en/wealth-management/uhnw/billionaires

-report/_jcr_content/mainpar/toplevelgrid/col2
/actionbutton.0564736741.file/bGluay9wYXR
oPS9jb250ZW50L2RhbS9hc3NldHMvd20vZ2xv
YmFsL2RvYy91YnMtYmlsbGlvbmFpcmVsVWl
uc2lnaHRzLTIwMTkuGRm/ubs-billionaires
-insights-2019.pdf.

2. "Shark Tank Stars Mark Cuban and Sara Blakely Tell
   Us How They Got to Their First $1 Million—And
   How You Can, Too," *Money,* August 14, 2017, https://
   money.com/mark-cuban-sara-blakely-interview
   -how-to-get-rich/.

3. "#179: Mark Cuban," *Forbes,* January 26, 2020,
   https://www.forbes.com/profile/mark-cuban/#75
   c3c6236a04.

4. "Shark Tank Stars Mark Cuban and Sara Blakely,"
   Money.

5. Ibid.

6. "#23: Sara Blakely," *Forbes,* January 26, 2020, https://
   www.forbes.com/profile/sara-blakely/#19cc
   fcf176bb.

7. Randall Lane, "Warren Buffett's $50 Billion Deci-
   sion," *Forbes,* March 26, 2012, https://www.forbes
   .com/sites/randalllane/2012/03/26/warren-buffetts
   -50-billion-decision/#516c85cb40cb.

8. "#3: Warren Buffett," *Forbes,* January 26, 2020,
   https://www.forbes.com/profile/warren-buffett
   /#6e1edae46398.

9. Lane, "Warren Buffett's $50 Billion Decision."

Index

9-to-5 job, 12, 42, 48
40-hour workweek, 12
401(k) employer matching
    program, 128–129
401(k) retirement plan, 4,
    75–76, 110, 125–126
    investment in, 129–130

A
after-hours trading, 113
after-tax income, 30–31, 34, 75
Amazon, 99
Apple, 99
artificial intelligence, 1, 3,
    26–27, 44, 52–53, 133,
    181
    companies transition, 7–9
    definition, 4–7
    gig economy and, 14–18
    impact on jobs, 5–6, 8–10,
    25, 28, 43, 174
    job creation, 6
    preparation for, 7–9
    tax, 55–57
    tax revenue losses, 126–127

B
balance transfer cards, 84–85
Bank of England (BOE), 122

Bank of Japan (BOJ), 122
Berkshire Hathaway, 100, 105,
    108–109, 130
Bill, Gates, 128
billionaires, 40, 177–180
    financial independence and,
    178–179
bond markets, 122–123
Branson, Richard, 5
Buffett, Warren, 100, 105,
    108–109, 130, 179–180

C
CAPEX, 158–159, 162–163
cash back rewards, 69
certificate of deposit (CD),
    47–48
Chief Executive Officer
    (CEO), 114
Chief Financial Officer (CFO),
    114
Chief Operating Officer
    (COO), 114
city's economy, 168
Coca-Cola, 99
company going public, 12–13
compound interest, 37–40
computer coding, 12
consumer spending, 119

cooking at home, 66
copyediting, 12
CoreLogic's Home Price Index, 169
cost of living, 3
COVID-19 outbreak, 27, 118
credit card
 debt, 72–73, 78–80
 discounts, 70–71
 interest, 80–82
 minimum payment, 58–59, 80–81
 with multiple balances, 82–84
 paying off debt, 82–83
 reward points, 68–71
 use, 57–60
credit score, 72–73
Cryan, John, 9

D
debt payments, 77
 credit card, 72–73, 78–84
 mortgage debt, 91–93
 student loan, 85–90
deflation, 119
disposable income, 30
dividends, 102–106
Dow Jones Industrial Average, 107

E
earnings reports, 111–114
eating out, 66
employee student loan debt, 90
"enough money," 3
entrepreneur, 17
European Central Bank (ECB), 122

F
Federal funds rate, 120
Federal Reserve, 119–121
financial crisis 2008, 107, 118, 121, 168
financial equation, 28–29, 92
financial independence, 1–3, 24–25, 30, 74, 78, 133, 174, 182. see also housing costs, ideas for reducing
 billionaires and, 178–179
 money required for, 46–51
 occupational change and, 17, 20
 types of, 41–46
financial responsibilities, 2
fixed income, 122
food delivery services, 16
freelance work, 12

G
gig economy, 11–14
Goldman Sachs, 17
government's jobs report, 116–117
government student loans, 87–90
graphic design, 12
groceries, 64–65
gross domestic product (GDP), 117–118

H
health-care costs, 44, 51–53
health insurance, 51–53
Home Depot, 99
homeowner's insurance, 155–156

housing costs, ideas for
    reducing, 133–134
    buying investment property,
        152–167
    finding cheaper apartment, 63
    finding cheaper
        neighborhood, 63
    live in one unit and rent out
        the other, 148–152
    mortgage interest, 140–145
    moving in with your
        significant other, 62–63
    renting vs buying, 134–138
    roommate, 62
    sunk costs of home
        ownership, 138–140
housing expenses, 61–64

I
IBM Institute for Business
    Value (IBV) study, 6
illiquid stocks, 111
income inequality, 177
income taxes, 30–31
index funds, 106–110
inflation, 49–50
interest rates, 73–74
investment property loans, 149

J
job displacement, 18

K
keep your day job, 43–46

L
labor resistance, 15
lease agreements, 165–166

liquid stocks, 110
loan repayment, 86–90,
    92
lower interest rates, 120–121
Lyft, 12–13

M
management fee of funds,
    129–130
Medicare, 21
Millennials, 3, 13, 95
million dollars, idea of,
    23–24
monthly nonfarm payrolls
    report, 116
mortgage, 155
mortgage debt, 91–93

N
national savings rate, 31, 35
neighborhood, 167–169
nest egg, 49

O
occupational change, 17, 20
opportunity cost, 92
owning a home outright,
    145–146

P
part-time job, 42–43, 62
passive income, 3
population growth, 168
premarket, 113
premium, 115
Procter & Gamble, 17
"produces income," 24
profit, 28–29

property
  buying investment,
    152–154
  cash flow, 163–165
  lease agreements, 165–166
  live in one unit and rent out
    the other, 148–152
  maintenance costs, 150–151
  managing, 150
  revenue from, 161–162
  selling, 151–152
  taxes, 157
  valuing, 154–161
property manager, 150

R
real estate investing, 173–175
refinancing of loan, 93
rental properties, 3, 147, 154,
  157
  short-term rentals,
    169–173
repairs, 158
reskilling, 26–27
retirement, 4, 98
retraining, 26
revenue, 29
rewards card, 67–68
robots, 5, 78
robot tax, 127–128
Roth IRA, 130–131

S
savings rate, 30–34, 36, 40, 49
  cooking at home, 66
  groceries, 64–65
  housing, 61–64
  increasing, 35–37, 39–40

self-driving car technology, 13,
  15
Shiller, Robert J., 144–145
short-term rentals, 169–173
  risks with, 170–173
skip the morning latte,
  66–67
Social Security, 21
S&P 500, 99–100, 106–109,
  129–130
start-up, 33
stocking up items, 64–65
stock market, 37, 48, 95–96,
  174
  dividends, 102–106
  economic data and, 116–118
  Federal Reserve policy and,
    119–121
  idea of return, 96–98
  index funds, 106–110
  reactions, 115–116,
    118–119
  retail sales, 118
  stock prices, 110–116
  ways to make money with
    stock, 100–106
  working of stocks, 98–100
stock prices, factors that impact,
  110–116
  corporate mergers, 115
  earnings reports, 111–114
  economic data, 115–116
  geopolitical conflict, 115
  government policy, 115
  government's jobs report,
    116–117
  gross domestic product
    (GDP), 117–118

retail sales, 118
supply and demand, 111
strong or weak earnings, 112
student loan
    debt, 85–86
    repayment, 86–87
Sundararajan, Arun, 13–22

T
tax deductions, 55–56
tax revenue
    losses from artificial
        intelligence, 126–127
    robot tax, 127–128
tenant's security deposit,
    166–167
tracking expenses, 57–61
two-unit property, 148, 152

U
Uber, 12–13, 15
unemployment, 27, 168, 174
universal basic income (UBI),
    20–22
utilities, 156–157

V
valuing property, 154–161

W
Wall Street, 112–113
water bill, 156
withdrawal of money, 49–51
writing, 12

Y
Yang, Andrew, 8